LAST BARRIER TO FREEDOM

Internment of
Jewish Holocaust Survivors
on Cyprus, 1946-1949

By Morris Laub

Judah L. Magnes Museum
2911 Russell Street
Berkeley, California

Cover design by Sara Glaser
Typeset by Heyday Books

Published by the Judah L. Magnes Museum
2911 Russell Street
Berkeley, California 94705

ISBN: 0-943376-25-4
Library of Congress Catalogue Card: 84-82475

10   9   8   7   6   5   4   3   2   1

LAST BARRIER
TO FREEDOM

E R R A T A

Last Barrier to Freedom

P. 28, paragraph 3:
Read Central Committee
for Control Committee

P. 64, paragraph 4:
Read while we conversed in Hebrew
for while he conversed in Hebrew

P. 65, paragraph 2:
Read the Palestinian newspaper
for the Cyprus camps' newspaper

P. 72, paragraph 5:
Add In addition, I planned the *seder*
to be held outdoors for all the . . .

To the memory of my late wife, Eve.
And to our two sons, Levi Lee and Marc Menahem.
They made our home an island of normality
amidst the tears and joys of our brothers and sisters
who were forced to languish behind barbed wire
on the fair island of Cyprus.

ACKNOWLEDGMENTS

I wish to thank the American Jewish Joint Distribution Committee and its executive vice-president, Ralph Goldman, for placing the resources of this foremost rescue operation at my disposal, for encouraging me to write about my experiences, and for making possible the realization of this idea.

Also to Rose Klepfisz, the able and dedicated archivist, who opened the JDC archives for me and guided me through them.

My sincere thanks to the Memorial Foundation for Jewish Culture for its grant and to its executive vice-president, Dr. Jerry Hochbaum for his help.

To the Judah L. Magnes Museum, and its indefatigable and imaginative director, Seymour Fromer, goes my deep appreciation.

To Sara Glaser, also of the Magnes Museum, my profound thanks for designing and producing this book.

Table of Contents

INTRODUCTION

Last Barrier to Freedom reflects one of the most disheartening aspects of the immediate post-Holocaust period as well as one of the most heroic affirmations of the human spirit. The shameful fact that the desperate survivors of the Nazi death camps, the remnant of European Jewry, were not welcomed anywhere or assisted to migrate to the haven of their choice, but, instead, had to resort to dangerous "illegal" immigration, is compounded by the establishment of yet another forced detention camp for them. Those who were removed from the densely-packed refugee ships that were attempting to reach the shores of Palestine must have felt that even after Hitler, the civilized world cared little about their fate. That the allied nations stood by for the further humiliation of the Jewish survivors of Naziism, helps us to understand the determination of those who worked to assure that such powerlessness would never again be possible. One would expect that the 55,000 detainees on Cyprus would be so demoralized that they would be hopeless and unable to function. Morris Laub, who as Cyprus director for the American Jewish Joint Distribution Committee was in a unique position to be both participant and observer, shows us that, miraculously, the opposite was true. We learned that the survivors retained their hope and determination. With the help of world Jewry, and especially of the Jewish community of Palestine, they organized themselves for education, culture, family life, military service and settlement in the land of Israel. The close cooperation between all elements of world Jewry, and non-Jews, to help the survivors, represents a heroic period in post-war Jewish history.

We are grateful to Morris Laub for giving us this vital record of what has become a little-noted or remembered phase of the events after the Holocaust and of those leading to the creation of the State of Israel. The Magnes Museum is proud to publish this volume as well

ix

as to present a comprehensive exhibit on life and art in the Cyprus detention camps, which was inspired by this book. It is our hope that this volume will evoke further research, exhibits and public interest in the Cyprus experiences. We are most grateful to Sara Glaser, who prepared the book for publication and designed its cover. We are appreciative of the grant from the Joint Distribution Committee which made this publication possible. Many thanks go to Malcolm Margolin and the staff of Heyday Books. We appreciate, as well, the consultation and assistance of Ruth Eis, Nelda Cassuto and the staff of the Magnes Museum. We gratefully acknowledge the contributions of Naftali Bezem and Louis Laub to this book.

Seymour Fromer
Director
Magnes Museum
November 15, 1984

LAST BARRIER
TO FREEDOM

The Western World in August, 1946

The Cyprus camps opened on August 14th, 1946, a year after the end of World War II.

The postwar world was full of reminders of the war for both the victors and the vanquished.

Millions of people lost their lives. The total figure for Russia alone is estimated to be 20 million. Dozens of cities had been bombed into obliteration, though here and there a major city escaped, having been declared an "open city"—Rome, for example, or Paris.

Food was scarce, prices were high, and one kept wondering how people lived. Those of us who were in the United States Army or wore uniforms—as American Joint Distribution Committee Personnel did, though we were not army men—received special treatment. We had cigarettes available; they were the currency of the day; a pack would at times buy as much as a suit of clothes. It was not unusual to see people in Paris picking up butts, which would then be remade into cigarettes with newspaper, as cigarette paper was scarce.

When I discovered that the condition of a person's shoes was often a quite accurate indication of his or her situation, it became an almost instructive habit to look at people's shoes, a habit that stayed with me when I visited Europe again some years later.

As for the political situation, though the United Nations had been established in 1945 in San Francisco, and though the victors, no longer afraid of the dreaded Gestapo or of Nazi bombings and terrors against civilian populations, established what they hoped were ongoing democratic regimes, there were many discouraging conflicts. Thoughts of unity and resistance to the enemy slowly dissipated into antagonism, rivalry, and even hostility among the political parties; stable regimes were rare. The only really stable regime seemed to be in the USSR, and there the stability must be ascribed to the absolute hegemony of the Communist Party.

1

The Marshall Plan, conceived by General Marshall and brought into being by President Truman, was instituted and millions of dollars began pouring into all countries that were ready to accept the terms of the plan. Even Russia had been invited to do so, but refused, harboring suspicions on the designs of its former allies. The Marshall Plan was slow to take effect; the summer of 1946 still saw Europe and North Africa suffering from the ravages of war.

Six million Jews were lost in the Holocaust: a third of the Jewish world population destroyed, a proportion unmatched by that of any other nation. In addition, the destruction of a thousand-year-old culture dominant in Russia, and especially in Poland, accompanied the horror of the physical destruction.

Jews had lived in Poland and Russia for a millenium; Yiddish was the main language of prayer and study, while Polish, Russian and Ukranian, German, and other Western languages were also the languages of the Jewish intelligentsia in those countries.

Yeshivas (academies of high Jewish learning), Yiddish universities, and all kinds of lower schools were destroyed. Newspapers were wiped out, including famous papers read by Jews throughout the world, such as *Hajnt*, *Moment*, and others. Book publishers, who had been instrumental in bringing to the mass of Jews the fruits of the renaissance of Yiddish and the works of the masters, no longer existed.

At war's end, the many Jews who were in concentration camps were liberated by American and other foreign troops. General Eisenhower was among the first to see the living skeletons in the camps and he wept at the sight.

The survivors left for home. For some, home meant Poland again, or perhaps Russia; for many others, home meant Palestine. These, whether they had been Zionists or not before the war, had come to the realization that Europe and its horrors was no longer the place for them—that only Palestine would welcome them and provide for their children's future.

Some of those who went back to Poland came either from Western Siberia or Russia, where many Jews had been saved from the concentration camps. They intended to stay, and began rebuilding their lives; however, the pogrom of Kielce on July 4, 1946 changed their minds and made them decide once and for all to leave Poland. If, after the war, such a pogrom could take place in a city of Poland,

Passengers from an "illegal" boat being transferred at Haifa to British Naval vessel for deportation to Cyprus.

On board a refugee boat.

which now presumably was run by a government friendly to Jews, then what could one expect? So, goodbye to Poland. They were on their way to Palestine.

They were led by the *Bricha*, the *Mossad*, and the *Aliya Bet*. The *Mossad* was the Jewish intelligence organization in Palestine which organized help for the Jews during the war and arranged immigration to Palestine after the war period. According to the terms of the British White Paper of 1938, this immigration was limited to 75,000 Jews over a period of ten years, a figure ridiculously low in the eyes of the many more thousands who clamored to go. And so *Aliya Bet* came into being for the so-called illegal immigration.

All kinds of boats were used: some rickety and some sturdy, 200 tonners as well as 4,500 tonners, carrying as few as 200 passengers per boat to as many as several thousand. Some of them were overcrowded, with as many as 7,500 passengers to a boat as it risked the hazardous journey across the Mediterranean. The ports of embarkation were usually in Italy, and there, under the guidance of Yehuda Arazi—known to everyone as "The *Zaken*" (old man), though he was not—the trips to the boats and then to Palestine were organized. The word "organized" comes easily to the lips, but this involved months of planning and work: setting aside places for lodging, getting the necessary trucks, gaining cooperation from the Italians who were friendly to the Jewish cause, and, above all, building the boats.

The Jewish world was not limited, of course, to Jews in Europe or Palestine; it included Jews in America. They rallied in response to the calls of the United Jewish Appeal, whose primary aim was to bring aid to Jews already in Palestine and to those who wanted to get there.

Fantastic sums, tens and later hundreds of millions of dollars, were pledged and donated annually by Jews of America and Canada and other such free nations as South Africa and England. This not only showed solidarity but also told the world that Jewish history is eternal, that Jewish life must go on, that even the Holocaust could not stop Jews from surviving and upholding their culture, their religion and their contribution to the world.

My Association with the
American Jewish Joint Distribution Committee
and My First Task on Cyprus

I was asked to go to Cyprus by the American Joint Distribution Committee, for which I had been working abroad since I joined the organization in July 1944. My assignments abroad included one in Italy between the fall of 1945 and the spring of 1946, which brought me in contact with Palestinians in the Jewish Brigade of the British Army.

I quickly established a rapport and worked closely with them on various matters including *Bricha* (flight or movement) and *Aliya* (immigration).

In August 1946, Britain's Foreign Minister Ernest Bevin initiated his policy of deporting Jews who came to Palestine in contravention of the White Paper. Having failed to stop immigration, Bevin decided upon a policy of deportation to Cyprus, which is about 200 miles from Palestine—one hour by air, overnight by boat. The deportations came as a shock to the entire *Yishuv* (Jewish community of Palestine). Protests mounted throughout the world against Bevin's latest device.

As soon as the camps were opened, the American Joint Distribution Committee in Palestine, under the direction of Charles Passman, asked for permission to go to the camps on Cyprus to see what could be done for the incarcerated Jews.

Formed in 1914, the American Joint Distribution Committee, known as the JDC in the United States and as "The Joint" everywhere else in the world, is the largest Jewish relief organization. It had provided relief, rehabilitation, and rescue for Jews throughout the First World War and the postwar periods in Europe and it was now engaged, with its traditional efficiency, in bringing help to Jews caught by the Second World War in Europe and elsewhere.

5

My work in the JDC made me realize that it was a unique organization; it satisfied me completely in my search for a way to do something for Jews caught in the war. My work in Italy strengthened my determination to remain with the JDC as long as possible, so that I could continue to help Jews to the best of my ability.

When the camps were first opened on Cyprus, nobody expected them to last much longer than a few months. It was in this expectation that Rose Viteles, a Jerusalemite originally from the United States, was asked by the JDC in Palestine to go to Cyprus and see what could be done for the Jews in the camps. Ms. Viteles stayed about two months and had to return home to Jerusalem.

It was at this point that I was asked by Mr. Passman and the JDC in New York to go to Cyprus. I was told that I had been specifically asked for by the Palestinians because they knew me and trusted me; also, I was at home in Hebrew and could communicate with them easily. With the expectation still high that the camps would close very soon, I was assured by the JDC that I would not have to stay longer than a few months. I left New York and arrived on Cyprus on December 10, 1946. The expected few months turned into years; I stayed until February 18, 1949.

I shall never forget the very first incident in which I was involved as the Country Director of the JDC on Cyprus. One of the "illegal" boats was the *Rafiah*. On its way across the Mediterranean to Haifa or another port in Palestine where it was the hope to secretly unload its several hundred passengers, it ran into rocks near Greece and was smashed to bits. All the passengers were rescued by a British naval boat, except eight persons who drowned. A British boat brought its 785 passengers, who were kept down in the hold and guarded by British sailors, directly to Cyprus.

When they arrived they refused to leave the hold, claiming that this was not where they had intended to go and that the boat must take them to Palestine. The captain of course refused and pleaded with them to leave. The Jews were adamant. When I was asked by the captain to go down to the hold and talk to them, I agreed. I was admitted into the hold and spoke in Yiddish to the several hundred Jews, telling them how futile it was at this point to insist upon their demands or to try to resist. I advised them to give up and allow themselves to be transported to a camp. They booed and hissed at me. They mocked and called me an agent of the British. They branded me as a traitor. I left saddened, wondering what their fate would be.

Their fate was immediately resolved. Tear gas was used. When they came out coughing and crying, they were herded into British lorries and transported to one of the camps.

That incident has been with me all these years. There I was, brought over to Cyprus to help the Jews, and yet I found myself called a "spokesman" for the British. That incident has made me realize that occasionally one does something in the course of one's duties that seems to be antithetical to one's real position—and even unethical.

Was I a British agent? Of course not. Yet I was their "spokesman". Should I not have been their spokesman? Knowing that in one way or another the Jews would be forced out of the hold, didn't my position compel me to do what I could to help, even though at that moment I seemed to act as a spokesman and was denounced as an agent by Jews whom I came to help?

I have been thinking about this all these years. Whenever I hear or read about a situation similar to mine, I remember my own role in the *Rafiah* incident and avoid making immediate judgments.

Another part of the *Rafiah* experience that has remained with me is my meeting with Dr. Haim Schieber, later known as Dr. Sheba. Dr. Sheba flew out to the island on which the *Rafiah* was smashed, saw that eight Jews had been drowned, helped to give immediate medical attention to the survivors, and picked up remnants of their belongings floating in the water. He then proceeded to Cyprus and we got to know each other. He showed me moistened pages of prayer books which he had found afloat. To him they were the symbol of Jewish eternity.

As I got to know him, Dr. Sheba became the symbol to me of the complete Jew and the complete doctor. For Dr. Sheba, no Jew was alien. Religious observances, party affiliations, class distinction—none of these tempered his regard for Jews. The ancient words *kol Yisrael haverim* (All Jews are united in fellowship) had real meaning for Dr. Sheba and determined his actions.

When I first met him on Cyprus he was associated with the *Haganah* (the resistance); later he became the chief medical man in the Israeli Army. He subsequently organized Tel Hashomer, which is now the Sheba Hospital, one of the foremost hospitals in modern

7

Israel focusing on rehabilitation medicine. Whenever I have a moment of despair or a feeling of futility, I think of Dr. Sheba and my spirits are lifted immediately; the blackness of the moment departs and I am able to resume my activities. I am fortunate that Dr. Sheba and I became friends. He was one of the great men of my life; thinking of him has always spurred me on to do my best in any task I was engaged in.

Another Boat that Foundered

Of the 39 boats whose passengers were deported to Cyprus, all except four landed in Haifa. The four included the *Rafiah*, the *Shabtai Lozinsky* and the *Pan* ships. On March 13, 1947, a shipload of *Aliya Bet* immigrants tried to avoid landing in Haifa and risking deportation to Cyprus. Instead, the *Shabtai Lozinsky* headed for a southern point of embarkation and almost made it, but like the *Rafiah*, it foundered on rocks; unlike the *Rafiah*, it suffered no casualties. Palestinian Jews watching from the shores for the boat saw the accident and immediately tried to rescue the passengers.

They swam to them, went out on rowboats and small motor boats and any other available craft and succeeded in bringing in many persons. The British, too, were alerted and sent lorries to round up everybody that was brought in, so that together with the rescued *Aliya Bet* immigrants, many subjects of Palestine were included in the roundup.

This mixed group, immigrants and Palestinians, was hurried northward to Haifa, transferred to a British naval vessel and brought to Cyprus.

The scene that accompanied the arrival of this new group of *ma'apilim* (Cyprus deportees) remains fixed in my mind. Because so many were Palestinians, they had friends on the JDC staff who eagerly awaited them. When they met, there were touching moments of welcome: kissing, embracing, and the exchange of news from home. This of course did not in any way hinder the usual welcome given to new arrivals. They were settled into various camps in Caraolos and, like all other *ma'apilim*, began their sojourn for an indefinite period of time.

The transfer of Palestinians who were not "illegal" immigrants to Cyprus raised immediately a serious legal question. How could the Palestinian government take its subjects and deport them? The Mandate Government was very much aware of this problem and began quickly to resolve it. The liaison between the British in Cyprus and myself was at that time Tony Aldridge, a young, affable diplomat with whom I had a rapport and a sort of friendly relationship. He knew his role; I knew mine. We both understood that although we were in a sense antagonists, we were, so to speak, in the same boat. We were both responsible for tending to the needs of the internees—he from the British point of view and I from the Jewish point of view.

Aldridge was also troubled by the arrival of the Palestinians and he was besieged by reporters with urgent questions about the government's plans. He dared not say to the reporters that he honestly did not know anything. A day or two after the arrival of the Palestinians, Aldridge and I were having a drink in the bar of the Hotel Savoy in Famagusta, and in all innocence he turned to me and said, " Morris, tell me, how many came from Palestine?" I did not know, but I did know that I had to make up a figure and that I had to exaggerate. Sending the Palestinians back, which was the first order of priority for the Mandate Government, might have the happy effect of forcing the government also to send some genuine newcomers to Palestine, mistaking them for Palestinians. With this in mind, I said, "Tony, I honestly don't know, but my educated guess would be at least 300." He gasped.

I am sure he reported that number back to his authorities in London, Nicosia, and Jerusalem.

Suit was brought against the Mandate Government by the Jewish Agency because of the deportation of Palestinians. The government then decided to send an experienced police officer, Captain Marner, to check on all those who claimed to be Palestinians, and to sort out the real Palestinians from any impostors. Captain Marner came with a Jewish interpreter. While he knew Palestine well, and even a little Hebrew, he really did not know Hebrew well enough to carry on the investigation.

I never knew the name of the interpreter, but he rendered a great

9

service, for he tipped us off that Captain Marner could be "persuaded" to send more than the correct number. This confirmed what some of the Palestinians already knew about him, namely that he could be "bought," and bought he was: three suits of clothing made to order and 50 pounds as well.

Marner announced that he would begin his investigation of the Palestinians approximately ten days after his arrival. The next ten days are also etched in my memory because the true Palestinians, the JDC staff and the *Shabtai Lozinsky* arrivals sat down in small groups with men, women, and children, all of them newcomers, in an attempt to have them learn as much as possible about Palestine.

The details that could confirm one's alleged Palestinian residence were everyday details and the answers to everyday questions had to be learned: What newspapers were published? What bus do you take in Tel Aviv from the Mograbi to Ben Yehuda and Keren Kayemet streets? What movie did you see last week or when was the last time you went to the movies? In what theater did it play? Where do you do your shopping? How much is a quart of milk? These were the kinds of questions asked. I watched the endless drilling in an attempt to get these daily matters so fixed in the minds of the learners that an automatic instantaneous answer would come to their minds.

Certainly, one had to know the coinage system and therefore all the coins and bills in Palestine currency were shown to the internees. In those days, some of the coins of smaller denominations had a hole in them, so "mit a lekhele, un on a lekhele" (with a hole, without a hole) became an intense subject of discussion. It made me laugh, but of course I realized that such mundane matters could determine an internee's ultimate destination—Cyprus for an indefinite stay or Palestine today. The day came when Captain Marner and his interpreter sat down to carry on the examination. He asked some of the very questions we anticipated and others that we hadn't. Generally speaking, he was easy on them and let many more go than should really have been permitted. Actually, about 140 Palestinians had come, and about 325 passed muster and left Cyprus.

Some of the Palestinians did not present themselves for examination, among them some members of the *moshav* Kfar Warburg. They decided to remain in Cyprus and help the others.

The authorities of course did not know this, because those who had been deported from the *Shabtai Lozinsky* and their Palestinian rescuers lived together with the other internees. I talked to one of the men at about 7 A.M. one morning about his *moshav* and about the rescue of the smashed boat. He had swum out and brought in a number of persons.

"Why did you do this?" I asked.

"Isn't that a silly question?" he answered. "What else should I have done—stood by and watched them drown?" Then he went on to say with a smile, "You know, it is wonderful here."

"Wonderful?" I asked.

"Yes," he continued. "Do you realize that this is the first vacation that I have had in many, many years?"

"Vacation?"

"Yes. Here I don't have to get up at 4 A.M. in the morning to milk the cows. I don't have to pursue my other chores. I don't have to worry about what's happening out in the fields. I have nothing to do here. It's a vacation."

Vacation or no, many Palestinians wanted to remain. They had a compulsive need to help the internees. And one of the first ways to help was to teach them to keep the camp clean. A *moshavnik* to whom cleanliness on his farm is second nature simply couldn't tolerate the dirt in the camps. Therefore, cleaning up became task number 1. Number 2 was the volunteering of their services to help the staff fix up our warehouse and organize it. Number 3 was to instill in the internees the spirit of Zionism as they, the *moshavniks*, felt it, to tell about the *Yishuv* as they knew it, and to describe to the *ma'apilim* what awaited them upon their arrival in Palestine.

The volunteers had to obtain permission from Kfar Warburg, which was readily granted. The average Palestinian's desire to be of help to the unfortunates in Cyprus was fulfilled.

The *Pan Crescent*.

The *Pan York*.

The Two "Largest Boats Ever"

Two other boats in addition to the *Rafiah* and the *Shabtai Lozinsky* came directly to Cyprus without the forced debarkation at Haifa and transfer of passengers to British naval vessels: the *Pan Crescent* and the *Pan York*, which arrived on January 1, 1948, at the port of Famagusta. On Decembr 31, 1947, New Year's Eve, a few of us sat in my house in Famagusta, celebrating the New Year. We drank a little and sang a little and talked a lot; as usual the talk was about Cyprus, the camps, the people, and the eternal question: when will they be released?

I went to bed long after ushering in the New Year. A few hours later I was awakened by Levi, my nine-year-old son, who said in a very excited voice, "Daddy, Daddy, the two largest boats ever are in the Famagusta harbor. Hurry, get up!" Levi, who would often ride on his bicycle early in the morning, had just returned from a visit to the harbor.

I quickly arose and rushed to the port. Sure enough, there were the two largest boats ever—the *Pan Crescent* and the *Pan York.* Together they brought 15,169 men, women and children. Their captains were two young men, Ike Aronowitz, 24 years old, and Gad Hilb, 27. Despite their youth they were seasoned and fearless men. In fact, Ike had been the captain of the renowned *Exodus*, whose odyssey had made the front pages of the world press for weeks.

These two ships, each 4,500 tons, were former freighters. They had left Constanza, Rumania, and later a port in Bulgaria and had made their way to Haifa. In the middle of the Mediterranean they were intercepted by the British and ordered to proceed directly to Cyprus. The captains refused and communicated with their superiors, the *Mossad*, who ran all of *Aliya Bet*.

Gad and Ike were advised to accede to the British commands, but only after negotiating an amicable method of debarkation. It took

13

quite some doing on the part of his superiors to convince Ike; his attitude was "To hell with the British. I'll do what I want." Discipline prevailed, however, and the boats came directly to Cyprus.

That was what greeted my eyes upon arrival that New Year's morning: two large boats, larger than any that I had seen or expected in Famagusta, and thousands of refugees on the decks waving, greeting people they knew, yelling, and weeping in relief. At last they were on safe ground.

The amicable debarkation which the British had negotiated with the captains meant no search of belongings, no bodily frisking, none of the pilfering that usually took place when passengers of an illegal boat were transferred at Haifa to a British naval vessel on its way to Cyprus.

It took the JDC staff eighty-four hours around the clock to disembark the passengers and register them. Registration simply meant a name, a party affiliation and some other details. Among those who disembarked were sailors known to some of our staff but unknown to the British; they gave names like George Washington, Abraham Lincoln, Charles DeGaulle, Yekum Purkan (the opening words of Hebrew prayers recited on the Sabbath) and Alenu Leshabeiakh (the closing prayer of every service).

The British complained to me, "How can a man be named George Washington?" I answered, "Why not? Besides, suppose it isn't his name; what do you want me to do? That's the name he gives and that's the name you have to register him by."

Ike Aronowitz was a well-known figure to many of my staff, especially to my deputy, Josh Leibner. When Ike disembarked, he ran toward Josh with open arms. Josh, not wanting the British to recognize their friendship, turned away. For a moment Ike was bewildered, but then understood and stopped his hearty welcome.

The *Pan* ships doubled our population overnight. Beginning with the first week in January 1948, we had 32,000 persons in the camp; we needed immediately additional personnel. Dozens of new teachers, doctors, nurses, and others were dispatched from Palestine.

On the ships were many who could be pressed into service as volunteers. Forty-eight doctors came, among them important surgeons—most important of all, Dr. Harden Ashkenazi. Many teachers, writers, and artists also came, some of whom have since become well known, even world famous.

14

Most of the passengers were Rumanians, and there were over a thousand Hungarians and 400 Bulgarians. The Rumanians were by and large a new element: among them was a group with strange, perhaps even criminal, tendencies. For the first time in the camp, brothels were set up. As soon as the emissaries got wind of this, the brothels were demolished and the heads of the prostitutes were shaved, a punishment known in those years for its use by members of Resistance movements against female collaborators with the Nazis.

The Bulgarians, 400 sturdy, healthy youths, seemed to be all Communists. Every day they marched and sang a song whose opening words I cannot forget: "Tito, Stalin, Dimitrov". They were a wonderful group of young people, and when they went to Palestine they eventually joined the Army and became good and active Israeli citizens.

The Rumanians, by contrast, represented the most bourgeois group that had ever been brought to the island. I sent a special report to the JDC about their bourgeois traits and trades. Other *Pan* passengers were Hungarians, who were largely adherents of the *Satmar Hasidim*, an extreme right-wing orthodox group which would have no contact with any other Hasidic groups—or any other Jews for that matter. They insisted upon their own *shekhita* (ritual slaughter) by their own slaughterers rather than by the *shokhet* (ritual slaughterer) sent to us by the Chief Rabbi of Palestine. The *shokhet*, together with a number of slaughterers whom he found in the camp, would go once or twice a week to Nicosia to slaughter cattle for kosher consumption. The British Army provided the lorries and facilitated all arrangements.

When the *Satmar* group refused to eat their meat because they would not recognize the authority of the Chief Rabbinate and demanded their own slaughterer, I was placed in a dilemma, troubled by the fact that I had to report to Sir Godfrey Collins, the British liaison. I didn't want to expose these differences among Jews to Sir Godfrey.

However, when he heard my story he quickly allowed the *Satmar* to have their own slaughterers, and also arranged for their slaughterers to go once or twice a week to Nicosia. I wondered about Sir Godfrey's quick and positive response until it dawned upon me that he was acting in the true spirit of the British colonial servant. He had been in the Indian Service of the British and brought with him all the knowledge and strategy that had to be employed with colonial peoples. If divide and rule—the classic method of colonialism and imperialism—were to succeed, it was important not to fuss about religious differences. This is precisely what Sir Godfrey did in our case. He instantly resolved my dilemma.

Dr. Harden Ashkenazi, Rumania's leading brain surgeon, had studied abroad and had acquired international fame. How the Rumanians permitted him to leave remains a mystery to me to this day; but he did leave, together with his family and his surgical instruments. Word got out somehow to the press that he was aboard one of the boats, but we were told that he would not leave the ship without his instruments. Despite the agreement between captains Ike and Gad and the British authorities, his refusal to disembark without the instruments worried us. We feared that Dr. Ashkenazi's suspicions might turn out to be right after all, and that his instruments would be confiscated.

Josh Leibner took it upon himself to go up on the boat to reach the doctor and to bring the instruments down. As soon as Josh came off the boat, so did the Ashkenazis.

With so many people in the camp, and everyone wanting to leave as quickly as possible, the Central Camp Committee, together with the emissaries, had instituted a policy which was largely followed: first in, first out. To some, it meant a wait of as long as 18 months. However, with the committee's approval and at the request of the emissaries, exceptions were occasionally made. One exception was Dr. Ashkenazi, who was to leave as soon as possible because Palestine, aflame with war, was in dire need of a brain surgeon. Other surgeons were also permitted to go without waiting for their turn.

Before leaving, each of the doctors, including Dr. Ashkenazi, was officially sworn into the *Haganah*. I was asked to be a member of the three-man commission who did the swearing in. I regarded this request as a great honor, but pointed out that, as I was a United States citizen, I probably had no right to do so. However, my hesitation gave way to my desire to accept the honor, and, with the other two members of the commission, I administered the oath, making Dr. Ashkenazi a member of the *Haganah*.

He left camp in three or four weeks, at the first opportunity.

Dr. Ashkenazi's arrival on Cyprus was widely reported in the press. Shortly afterward, I received a letter from a Jew in Egypt, who said that he had heard of Dr. Ashkenazi and wondered—in fact requested—that I intervene to have permission granted for the doctor to come to Egypt to operate on his son who was suffering from a brain tumor. He was ready to pay all expenses and guarantee Dr. Ashkenazi's safe return. I took the matter to Sir Godfrey Collins, who read the letter and turned down the request. Sadly, I informed the Egyptian father of my failure.

A few weeks later, after the doctor's departure, Sir Godfrey called me to his office and told me that a British soldier in Nicosia needed an urgent brain operation and that he would like to have Dr. Ashkenazi perform it. I informed Sir Godfrey that insofar as I knew, the doctor was no longer in the camp. "How is that possible?" he asked. "First in, first out—he should be here a long time."

I replied, "Please don't ask me how that's possible. You know I have nothing to do with these matters. You know the camps are run autonomously. The fact is, Dr. Ashkenazi is no longer here."

I was sorry for the soldier but I could not suppress a sense of satisfaction. "You didn't allow Dr. Ashkenazi to help a Jew," I said to myself. "Now he's not around to help your soldier."

The Camps and Their Organization

Who controlled the camps? Who made all the arrangements? What was the role of the British? What was the role of the JDC? Many such questions have been asked. This chapter will attempt to clarify most of them.

When Britain decided upon the plan for deportation, it selected Cyprus, a crown colony under British rule. Cyprus has had a checkered history with many different countries controlling it. Because of its location, near the shores of Palestine, Lebanon, Syria, and Turkey, it was throughout the centuries a kind of crossroads for clashing interests and fighting empires.

Jews seem to have always been on the island; at one time there were so many that they actually organized a rebellion against the ruling government. Then fate ruled that on August 14, 1947, Cyprus was to become the last Jewish concentration camp.

The camp known as Caraolos was situated approximately three miles from the city of Famagusta, one of six major cities in Cyprus. To make the camp ready for the reception of Jewish internees, tents were set up in Caraolos and the camp was encircled with barbed wire. Armed soldiers would guard the camps from watchtowers at various strategic points.

The Army had primary control and each camp had a major in charge, who reported in turn to a colonel who supervised the entire operation.

The Caraolos camps bore the numbers 55, 60, 61, 62, and 63. They were called the "summer camps" because of another set of camps in Dekhelia, eighteen miles from Caraolos, which came into being as the camp population grew. These Dekhelia camps did not have tents; they had Nissen huts, which were the equivalent of the American quonset hut, and they came to be called the "winter camps."

The Army, whose major responsibility was to care for the people and guard the camps, was not the only British element involved in the Cyprus operation. There were three others: the Colonial Office with headquarters in London, the British Mandate Government with headquarters in Jerusalem, and the government of Cyprus with headquarters in Nicosia.

While the interests of each were seemingly clearly delineated, there must have been differences of opinion and occasional clashes and controversy. It soon became clear that all four organs needed a liaison with the internees, and one was therefore appointed. First it was Tony Aldridge, then Mr. Smith, and finally Sir Godfrey Collins. The liaison person brought all his decisions, and occasionally problems of policy and administration to me, and I in turn brought to him our problems, demands, protests, and anything else we needed to express.

As soon as the camps opened, the Joint Distribution Committee in Palestine asked for permission to send a representative to see what it could do to help the internees. Permission was readily granted, and Charles Passman, Director of the JDC in Palestine, was the first representative. Mrs. Rose Viteles was then asked to come from

Jerusalem. Mrs. Viteles, a leading Hadassah personality and long-time Jerusalem resident, gladly accepted the invitation. When it became clear that the camps would not close, I was asked to take the position.

I arrived on December 10, 1946, and remained until the closing of the camps. Of course, I was not alone. I had deputies, a clerical staff of various grades, and other administrative help. In addition, we brought over doctors and nurses, teachers, educators, lecturers and all kinds of personnel necessary for the proper running of the camps. All of these people were direct JDC employees and I was their boss—or their supervisor.

Besides the direct JDC staff, there was another group of men and women who were not JDC employees, but emissaries of various kibbutzim and political parties in Palestine. They worked directly with the campers preparing them for life in Palestine and perhaps for membership in their respective parties. These people did not report to me, though in order to get into the camp they had registered with the authorities as JDC employees (nominal or quasi-JDC employees). Because my staff and I were in tune with them and they with us, we quickly established a rapport so that hardly anything went on inside the camp without prior knowledge and agreement on both sides.

There was a third group. Officially, I had nothing to do with it and made it known that I did not know about it. This was the *Haganah*, appointed by the leaders in Palestine to train and drill for whatever work (chiefly military) the *Haganah* did. Its people came over either as emissaries or as internees.

A fourth group was comprised of sailors and others who reported directly to the *Mossad*, which facilitated immigration to Palestine despite the limiting White Paper. The sailors were usually captured together with other internees and came to camp with them.

Finally, there was the Central Committee, the internal government of the camp, which represented and was composed of the campers themselves. Each part or grouping had a committee and all committees were represented in the Central Committee of the camp, which made policy based on discussion, debate, and agreement by the Central Committee with the cooperation of the emissaries. We in the JDC dealt with the Central Committee, which had the closest contact with us on all camp matters.

I regarded myself as the internees' spokesman before the British authorities. The Central Committee permitted me to do so because they had confidence in me and they trusted me—as they did all the JDC workers—since they recognized my devotion and commitment.

We worked literally from the moment we rose to the moment we went to sleep, generally from 6 A.M. until midnight (with breaks for meals and an occasional rest), seven days a week, for weeks and sometimes months on end. Once every three months a staff member would be given a week's leave in Palestine.

The British provided basic necessities. The Jews provided everything else, adding to the basics and making life possible during the long wait to leave. This was the makeup of the camp government.

The JDC Work

The camps at Cyprus were under the aegis of the JDC in Palestine for one reason: it was the only JDC operation (other than in Palestine) where Hebrew was the language of the administration. My entire staff consisted of Palestinians; we spoke Hebrew, they wrote reports in Hebrew and carried on meetings in Hebrew; everything was in Hebrew. No, not everything; the reports that I wrote to the JDC in New York and Paris were in English. And my contacts with the Central Comittee were conducted generally in Yiddish. Not everybody knew Hebrew well enough.

What did the JDC do? It provided supplementary food for everybody, especially women and children. It brought over doctors and nurses because the internees refused to be treated by the British. The doctors and nurses operated in the camps as well as in the Jewish wing of the British Military Hospital where all deliveries took place and where persons in need of hospitalization were sent. We had dentists and ophthalmologists, among others; we even had a team of psychologists and psychiatrists.

We were a complete medical operation—but those were the elementary things.

20

There was another elementary thing—clothing. In the summer camps (in Caraolos) the tent linings were used to make shorts. The results were baleful; the sun beat down mercilessly in the summer, and even the temperate winters to which Cyprus is accustomed were cool. The JDC supplied extra clothing, and tons of new and good used clothing were sent from New York.

These were the primary necessities; but people could not live on the bare necessities alone. They needed education, recreation, and cultural benefits. The JDC, with the aid of the *Youth Aliyah* and the Rutenberg Foundation, organized a complete school system—nursery schools, kindergartens, and elementary schools. For the adults, classes which they could attend during the day were held in Jewish history, customs and ceremony, and life in Palestine—all designed to prepare the internees for eventual release. But the weekend lectures were of the greatest interest to them. The speakers were superb. Week after week I would invite professors from the Hebrew University and other schools of higher learning, as well as political leaders and other persons of prominence, to spend a day or two and to talk about their special fields. The lecturers included cultural figures—great men and women of the Palestinian theatre, artists, poets, religious leaders—anyone who could bring enlightenment and hope to our needful internees.

However, even providing the necessities of culture was not enough. After all, it is not on bread alone that man lives, nor is it on bread and study together that the usual person lives. People needed vocations; and so we quickly decided to establish vocational schools in carpentry, plumbing, and other areas which could help the newcomer in Palestine land a job quickly.

However it took a long time before permission for workshops was granted, because to the British this meant the possession of tools, and the possession of tools meant a way to cut barbed wire and facilitate escapes.

I pleaded with the Army, which was sympathetic but helpless. I went to Cairo to plead, and presented the case for vocational training to the British Middle East Command. I was turned down. We bombarded the colonial office with requests. We were turned down. The rejections continued for months until, at last, after persistent demands, letters, wires, and interviews, the British finally gave in. The workshops were established. We had an additional ingredient to make life possible.

How long did the internee stay? The deal was "first in, first out" but, since only 750 were permitted to leave and thousands soon began to fill the camp, the length of stay had become extended—for some a few months, for others a year and a half . . .

Fortunately, the various activities helped the internees spend their time fruitfully, so much so that Cyprus became known as *Erev Yisrael*, the eve of Israel; which is to say that the people who stayed there were biding their time for the great day of release. Just as *Erev Shabbos*, the Friday before each Sabbath, is to every Jew a day of great preparation for the day of rest, contemplation, study, prayer, and family gathering—so was the bustling activity of Cyprus and the tension-filled anticipation of the eve of the "Great Sabbath" portending the great liberation, the great release, the final coming to Palestine.

Food, Clothing and Shelter

The British authorities provided food for the internees; however, that was not enough. They supplied bread, potatoes, vegetables, powdered milk, powdered eggs, margarine, tea, and meat which was sufficient only for Sabbaths—all in all about 2,100 calories per person daily. About 550 additional calories were given to pregnant women beginning with the 20th week of pregnancy. A British soldier received about 3,000 calories daily, and the average consumption of a British civilian, in the years of strict rationing during World War II, was about 2,800 calories daily.

The JDC immediately realized the insufficiency of the food upon beginning to work at the camps, and supplemented it with additional bread, potatoes, vegetables, fresh eggs, honey, oranges, and dates. Everyone received these, and children and pregnant women received even more. The service workers and *Haganah* trainees also received additional food. At the height of the population during 1948, the JDC spent about $30,000 a month for food supplements.

There were also canteens operated by the Central Commmittee

"Water." One from a series of linocuts by Caraolos camp internees portraying camp life.

where fruit, sewing materials, lux lamps, combs, bulbs for gasoline lamps, and other small items were sold at cost. Private enterprise in the form of canteens budded here and there but these were frowned upon. Because the internees were largely without money, relying on occasional gifts from friends and relatives outside the camp or on "official" money paid to workers by the JDC, the daily turnover at the end of 1947 for about 10,000 internees was $100.

Cyprus was constantly plagued by water shortages. Water had to be rationed, and would be brought in by lorry; however, sometimes the shortage was so severe that hours would go by—sometimes days—before it arrived. Impatience, resentment, and demonstrations resulted. The JDC tried to alleviate the situation as much as possible, but nature's elements were ultimately in control. The effects on cooking, washing, and sanitation were generally deleterious, especially when the sun beat down relentlessly during the spring and summer, the dry and hot seasons, with the temperature sometimes rising to 106 degrees. One of the most important functions of the "camp within a camp" was the daily provision of water which the JDC managed to scrounge.

Most of the internees boarded a boat with little besides what was on their backs, and that would often be lost or stolen or destroyed during the forced transfer to Cyprus-bound boats at the Haifa port. Upon arrival, behind barbed wire, each immigrant received a pair of shoes, two sets of underwear, some cloth, and a suit; or, for women, cloth for a dress and knitting wool. This was not enough and the first arrivals at Caraolos usually stripped their assigned tents of the blue cloth lining, which could be used for shorts and other light articles of clothing. There was a price which they had to pay for this. Others that came after them could do no stripping and all suffered in the cold because of the unlined tents, and, in the warm weather, because of the lack of lining to temper the rays of the sun. When Caraolos became full, other camps were set up and Nissen huts were used.

The JDC occasionally came to the rescue with the SOS program which managed to send many bales of clean, repaired, used, and even new clothes, which were, of course, much sought after.

One incident relating to the SOS program pointed out the clash of cultures between anonymous donors in the United States and anonymous recipients in Cyprus, when we received several thousand dark-gray striped work pants, all new and bearing the label of Lee, a well-known manufacturer of worker's clothes. I distributed them eagerly, but they were rejected. Some of the comments were: "Look what they're sending us, striped pants!" "What are we, diplomats? Who needs formal attire?" A pair of pants made for a worker in the United States was regarded as an article of dress for statesmen.

The Cyprus camps had two kinds of shelter: the tents in Caraolos and the Nissen huts of metal at Xylotymbou, the so-called winter camp. Each tent and hut had cots, mattresses, a pillow, and a gasoline lamp. There was no table, and no electricity or gas. That is why political party groups, and even some individuals who could afford it, acquired lux lamps.

What was particularly galling to the internee was that a separate prisoner-of-war compound made up of captured German prisoners did have electricity. Added to the bitter fact of enforced exile, the internee had to witness the sight of Nazis enjoying better living conditions.

The *"Haganah"*

In camp, the *"Haganah"* presided over all activities involving the boats, the sailors, the captains, and paramilitary training; they even attempted to structure the day-to-day governance of the camps. There were several bodies that actually spoke in the name of the *Haganah* and sometimes these bodies carried on internal discussion which emerged in internecine controversy, even strife, marked occasionally by conflicting orders and sometimes even by a refusal to obey orders. Most of us had no knowledge of these discussions. I certainly did not; for in camp there was a united voice, that of the *"Haganah."*

There was a *Mossad*, an *Aliya Bet*, a *Palmach*, emissaries, and a Central Committee.

The *Mossad* (Hebrew for "base, foundation, ground"), as the organization was known, was in charge of the overall illegal immigration policy and its implementation. It gathered those in Europe and elsewhere who clamored to go to Palestine, trained the people for the possible hazards that might force them to be captured by the British, and prepared them for their eventual arrival in the land of their desire: Palestine/Israel. The *Mossad* was organized in Palestine, staffed mainly by Palestinian Jews, and structured in a military manner which demanded discipline and obedience to orders.

The *Aliya Bet* (Hebrew for "Immigration B", an illegal immigration) was the arm of the *Mossad* for immigration activities. The vast variety of its work has caused it to be confused with the *Mossad*, which was broader, and included the *Bricha* (Hebrew for "flight"), the operation which arranged and mustered the flight of Jews from oppressor countries.

The *Palmach*, (literally, "striking force") largely comprised of *kibbutznikim*, was the fighting arm of the Palestinian Jews. After much strife, it was eventually integrated as *Zahal*, a Hebrew ac-

26

Opening of Campaign for Palestine Mobilization Fund, Caraolos,
Feb. 29, 1948. Top banner reads "Support the *Haganah*—you also
support your lives."

ronym for *Zva Haganah Le Yisrael* ("the Army for the Protection of
Israel"), organized by Ben-Gurion after statehood. In Cyprus, the
Palmach units accompanied the boats, sometimes running them,
and organized them against confrontation with the British; they even
made an attempt—quickly scotched by the internees—to run the
camps. It was rarely evident that the *Palmach* units were not always
in harmony with one another or with their superiors in Palestine.

The emissaries, presumably JDC employees, were organized by
the *kibbutzim* and political parties, and were in the various camps
for daily activity, all with a dual purpose: to help the internees and to
prepare them for eventual life in Palestine. Of course, party interests
were involved, but by and large the emissaries shared the overall
goal of preparing the internees for Palestine. They were respected
by the internees and their advice was sought.

It is interesting to observe that of all *Aliya Bet* operations, on
Cyprus and elsewhere in Europe, the Cyprus Central Committee
was the only one made up of internees themselves, who had ultimate
control of the final movement to Palestine. The Committee was
autonomous, yet often followed the wishes of the Palestinians as
represented by the various organizations that went by the magic
name, "*Haganah.*"

27

Political Parties

We had seventeen parties on Cyprus. Some were big, representing those in Palestine, and some were small splinter groups that had their genesis in Europe or in Palestine. The number seventeen was large in those days, even for Palestine, though that number may since have been equaled or even surpassed in other countries and in Israel. A parliamentary system with proportional representation makes that possible.

What were the functions of a party? First of all, they were ideological. Some were labor parties (Mapai, Hashomer Hatzair); some were religious (Agudas Israel, Mizrachi); some were worker-religious (Hapoel Hamizrachi); some were general Zionists (Noar Zioni); some revisionist (Betar); and others splinter groups of these. Mapai itself had two kibbutz movements represented on Cyprus. All of the parties preached their doctrines zealously to their adherents who were being prepared to enroll as members in good standing once they got to Palestine.

Another function was to have a place in the Control Committee, which was the policy-making and implementing arm of the autonomous government inside the barbed wire. Membership in the Control Committee was allotted by proportional representation, and the parties, by internal caucus, selected the representatives to the Central Committee, whose leader, or chair, brought its requests to the British and to the JDC. I very often was asked to speak for the Central Committee to the British, and gladly did so.

Decisions in the Central Committee were arrived at after a sometimes heated discussion. The frequent meetings served not only to ventilate ideas and shape policy, but also served as a therapeutic device to do something constructive with one's time and to develop leadership. The taste of politicking in the Central Committee was to the liking of some who became full-time or part-time politicians upon their eventual integration in Palestine.

28

"News." A party member broadcasts the day's news.

A third function of the party was thrust upon it by history. The party assisted in the rescue of the captives in Europe or North Africa, acted as a guide to Palestine and its people, represented the embodiment of Zionism, and served as a substitute family. The emissaries of the party, whether in the ghettos, fields and forests of Europe, or behind barbed wire on Cyprus, represented what came to be regarded as ideal people whose word was usually sought after, obeyed and respected. Only in the matter of the policy of first-in, first-out, did the internee himself prevail; but, here too some exceptions were made on the advice of the emissaries.

For many, the party acted as a surrogate father and mother. In fact, many were orphans and were especially dependent on the party.

Not everyone was in a party; some preferred not to be. But their lot was sad. They lacked a milieu in which they could socialize and play a part. Their independence exacted a price. Party adherents had their party as their family and society; the independents had independence and hardly anything else.

Independent by nature, I would have been a party adherent if incarcerated behind barbed wire under circumstances similar to those of the internee on Cyprus.

Attempts at Escape

Every prison is guarded for one reason—to prevent prisoners from escaping. Incarceration camps are also guarded and in Cyprus, as in every prison, there were attempts to escape.

All escapes were made from Caraolos because it was near the sea. Though Dekhelia was also near the sea, the escapes were concentrated in Caraolos because there were friendly persons near by. The Leibner home was one of the places in which an escapee could hide and the orange grove of Levinsky was another; there may have been one or two more.

It was the *Haganah* that would organize the escapes at the insistence of the *Mossad*. Sometimes in the dark of night, despite the incessantly sweeping searchlights and floodlights on the watchtowers, someone would get away. Occasionally a person would be brought out with a forged identity card. Lodging would have been pre-arranged where the escapee would await the hour when he was due to board a small clandestine vessel waiting to take him to Palestine. He would make his way, alone or accompanied by a *Hagannah* man, via a memorized route. Escapes were generally successful.

I recall, however, an unsuccessful one which had very unpleasant consequences. Cyprus had packs of dogs roaming the island in search of food. Unaccustomed to the attentions of human beings, they rarely seemed to become attached to people. However, many of these dog packs found their way into camp. The internees eagerly befriended and adopted them; the dogs, despite their semi-wild nature, became attached to individuals or families. One night, while an internee was trying to make his escape, a dog barked. It was immediately echoed by the barking of hundreds of dogs, and the escapee was caught. The next day an order came to kill all the dogs. I am sure that the partings were sad for both dogs and owners, but lives were at stake. Volunteers were called to do the killing, and a group from among the Sephardic contingent in camp came forth and strangled the dogs. It was a sad and depressing day. However, new herds of dogs soon found their way into camp and were, once again, adopted by internees. Occasionally someone would insist on taking his dog to Palestine, and generally the Central Committee allowed him to do so.

When the camps were finally closed, the dogs remained behind. It was very sad to see hundreds, perhaps thousands, of dogs roaming the camp in search of their masters. I discussed this problem with the British after the closing of the camps and they agreed to do something about it. What they did I had no way of knowing. I hope it was not as drastic as the previous solution.

Another method of escape was through a tunnel. I had an idea that a tunnel was being built, or perhaps had been built, but said nothing. Nobody told me; I preferred not to know. When the camps closed, I learned how the tunnel had been made. It was dug out under the cover of a tent which they filled with earth so that it would remain unseen by the watchtower guards. The tunnel, perhaps a

31

mile long, was built with ventilation so that the escapees could crawl through, occasionally sit down to rest, and continue on to a waiting boat. When the British and I took a final tour, I showed them the tunnel. In fact, it was the first time I had seen it myself. They inspected it very carefully and remarked that it was a feat of engineering the likes of which they had never seen. They asked me how many escaped and I invented a number well over 1,500—a grossly exaggerated number which was recorded in the press. Only 300 or so had made their escape through the tunnel.

Joshua Leibner

The most outstanding personality in Cyprus was my deputy, Joshua Leibner. He was the Palestinian *par excellence*, the embodiment of the kibbutz, a man with genuine concern for others. Some months after I came to Cyprus it became apparent that I needed a deputy. I asked Pessah Litwak (changed to Litav with the rise of the State of Israel), who was in charge of all Cyprus activities in the JDC office in Jerusalem, to find someone for me.

He suggested that I come to Jerusalem to meet Joshua Leibner. We hit it off as soon as we met. He was a kibbutznik, a member of the *Hashomer Hatzair* party, a leading personality in kibbutz Ein Hashofet, and a prominent person in the kibbutz movement. He was a former American and one of the founders of Ein Hashofet, which was then about twelve years old.

After a long conversation, I asked Josh to come to Cyprus; my first good impression remained. He threw himself into the work with a devotion I have rarely encountered. It was in fact a devotion to two ideals: one, his commitment in holding the post of Deputy Director of the JDC; and two, his desire as a kibbutznik to help the campers become good future Palestinians.

He was tireless. No task was unimportant or unbecoming to him. He was always ready to pitch in and, like all of us, he worked limitlessly—endless hours and days without a vacation. Josh quickly became my confidant and my most trustworthy counselor. It was with him that I explored any new idea that struck me. His opinions and advice weighed heavily and, more often than not, determined my actions.

Josh had received permission from Ein Hashofet to come and do this work and it became apparent that he would stay longer than expected. He asked me whether he could bring his family—his wife Pnina, his oldest son Ehud, and his daughter Ruth—and received permission from Ein Hashofet to do so. The Leibners were not new to missions for the Palestinian authorities. They had been to South Africa and they had been to the United States; now, they were in Cyprus.

The friendship with Josh was immediately extended to our families. Pnina and Eve, my wife, became close friends, and Ehud became Levi's closest friend. The boys studied with the same teacher, a tutor in the camp; Levi, motivated by his wonderful teacher, his great friendship with Ehud, and by the atmosphere of the camps, learned Hebrew quickly. The Leibners also lived in Famagusta and their home, like mine, became a place for all staff and emissaries to drop in and relax.

Though Josh was known as a *Hashomer Hatzair* leader, his devotion and idealism prevented his party affiliation from becoming a bar to help those of other parties. Everyone sooner or later realized that he was in Cyprus for one purpose—to help all Jews—and this awareness opened everyone's doors wide to him.

Being a Palestinian, Josh also learned many things I did not know—or did not want to know. He knew far more about the *Haganah* and the *Mossad* than I, because I really wanted to keep my hands clean so as not to compromise the JDC before the British authorities.

The *Haganah* and the *Mossad* people confided in him and he helped them. When plans for escape were in the making, Josh was in on them. Josh knew the tunnel was being built and I had just an inkling of the matter. When the Palestinians had to approach me with a matter they thought too delicate for me to become involved in, Josh became the liaison.

Besides being another home away from camp for staff and emissaries, Josh's home became a place for an occasional person to be brought secretly and hidden until escape to Palestine was made possible.

Left to right: Itzhak Yacobi, Rabbi Avraham Sjreibaum, Sir Godfrey Collins, Morris Laub, and Joshua Leibner on the occasion of the monthly quota departure of internees.

Officially, I knew nothing of these escapes, although I did have an inkling. Only once did Josh come to tell me that his home would be searched. He had been tipped off by a friendly British captain, Captain Maitland; acting on the tip, Josh got rid of the person being sought and the search turned out to be unsuccessful.

When Josh and Pnina finally left Famagusta, I knew that life would be difficult for us, especially for Levi who would lose his best friend Ehud. We therefore asked Ein Hashofet for permission to send Levi to live there until the camps closed. It was granted and Levi went. Therefore, my contact with Josh continued because the Leibners' became, in a sense, Levi's family. The Leibners became Levi's foster parents. We were eternally grateful to them and to Ein Hashofet for this act of fellowship. So was Levi; in fact my first grandchild, Levi's oldest son, was named Joshua after Josh Leibner, who died in 1952 or 1953.

A few years ago I was talking with Jacob Sjreibaum, who is now a high official in the Jerusalem Municipality and a troubleshooter and ombudsman for other communities (when Mayor Teddy Kollek can spare him). Mr. Sjreibaum served for about a year-and-a-half in Cyprus as the representative of the Immigration Authority of the Jewish Agency and of the Ministry of Immigration. He was at that time known as Rabbi Sjreibaum (he no longer uses his rabbinic title). He is a vigorous, witty, utterly upright human being. We got to talking about Cyprus and Sjreibaum talked a good deal about Josh Leibner. An Orthodox Jew, Sjreibaum called Josh a *tzadik* (a just man), the likes of whom he had never met. Yes, Josh was a just man, a rare man. His premature death remains an unforgettable loss to his family and friends.

Our Comptroller

I am now begining to tread warily, to "rush in where angels fear to tread." In the following chapters I will talk about a few members of the JDC staff. I do this with trepidation, for almost without exception every member of my staff deserves a description of his or her work and extraordinary devotion. To do so is of course impossible and I ask the forgiveness of those whom I omit. In presenting those that follow, I do not portray them only in their own right, but as symbols of the entire staff.

When I came to Cyprus, Itzhak Jacobowski (whenever I used the surname I could not help but think of "Jacobowski and the Colonel") was already there and he stayed on until the very end. Jacobowski —now Yacoby— was brought over from Palestine to undertake very important tasks. He organized the office. As the chief accountant and comptroller, he ran the books, supervised our purchases, supervised our warehousing, and kept track of the personnel records.

Itzhak and I quickly became friends. He was my right-hand man—the epitome of truth, honesty, and trustworthiness. Itzhak symbolized the highest ideals of his profession. All his tasks were performed in the same responsible manner. He steered a path between objectivity and subjectivity in dealing with the internees;

he kept the records, bought merchandise, and dealt with personnel straightforwardly, and also did whatever he could after hours in his overflowing empathy for the internees. "After hours" is the wrong expression for Itzhak. He had no hours. For many months he lived in camp, until at last he brought over his wife, Zilpa, and his child, Amnon (his daughter Tamar was born in Israel, after the camps were closed).

There was a silent understanding between us that was comforting to me. He stuck to the rules and occasionally I broke them. This was especially true in the matter of personnel when once in a while somebody wanted an extra week of leave or an extra day away from camp. Itzhak felt that permitting it would set a precedent for others, and refused. Invariably that person would come to me and usually I would consent. This image of Itzhak the "tough guy" and me the "softy" worked out well, and he never rebuked me, even by gesture, for doing something that he had denied.

His honesty was so ingrained that shady proposals which were sometimes made to him would upset him deeply. I recall him coming to me one day, terribly agitated, because our suppliers and vendors of fruits, vegetables and other necessaries had offered him a kickback. He wanted to break off relations with these suppliers. I inquired about this matter with a seasoned Cyprus person, the late Koenigsfeld (later Kingsfield of London), who owned orange orchards in Cyprus. With the opening of the camps, he and his wife associated with the JDC, first in a volunteer capacity and finally as employees. His wife Zillie told us that it would be foolish to refuse the kickbacks; that was simply the way of business in Cyprus. Learning this, Itzhak and I decided that he should accept them and turn them over to the JDC—in effect receiving a discount on our purchases. Later Itzhak was in charge of the special money which we issued; thousands of pounds went through his hands, all absolutely accurately accounted for, and all distributed in the equitable manner determined by us and the Central Committee.

On another occasion, a legitimate proposal was made to us. In a time of quick currency changes in Palestine, someone came with the idea that he would like us to act as his banker for Palestinian money to be converted into Cyprus money and thus insure that he would save his profits. He offered us a handsome percentage and even asked us to invest camp money and our own money if we wanted to do so. It was a perfectly legal proposal, but morally there was a stench about it. Itzhak and I refused. I recall now Itzhak's anger at this attempt to manipulate Palestinian money.

Our families became personal friends; such relationships on a closer level helped ease our common tasks. To this day we and the Yacobys have maintained our friendship, and to this day I recall him as the ideal associate.

A Social Worker Who Had No Clients, Only "Family" Members

Among those on the staff, there were also social workers. At the height of our population we had as many as four, all women, headed by Rivka Kahana. The social worker had the usual responsibilities that go with the profession, but the unusual nature of the camp brought on additional responsibilities, one of which was to buy things at the request of internees, who would pay for them. Such purchases were usually made in Famagusta.

The social worker tried to help make life more livable for the internees and to show them how to help themselves. But at no time did social workders attempt to have the internees adapt to life in the camp. There is a distinction between genuine adaptability and temporary adjustment and it was the latter which social workers tried to accomplish. Like the internees, they were infused with one desire: to have the camps close as quickly as possible, and like all of us, they worked towards that goal.

They also searched out particular personal problems, which might by chance have been overlooked by the medical staff. They were often psychological problems which could be treated easily, rather than psychiatric difficulties requiring professional help.

Rivka Kahana was a matronly woman in her forties. Her very presence exuded friendliness—a sense at times of being part of the family. She was like a sister to some, a mother to others, and a friend to all. Rivka and her staff would meet every Saturday morning at about 11:00 at my home for a weekly rundown of matters of particular concern and for planning for the next week.

The purely professional part of the work would be covered in a few minutes, and then Rivka would point out that one person needed a sweater, another a pair of shoes, another an extra blanket, and so on. We had a special sum of money for such purposes, but for Rivka it was never enough, and her requests were not those of the social worker about the camp, but those of a family member who had the good fortune to be free to go in and out of the camps.

I could not help being moved by Rivka's pleas, always accompanied by eloquent gestures and smiles, and almost invariably I overstepped the bounds of the budget. Though she realized that I could do no more, it was never enough for her, and so she would spend money out of her own pocket. When that came to my attention a few weeks later, I urged her to stop. She rebuked me gently, saying, in effect, that it was none of my business—if she wanted to help a family member, how could I stop her? For Rivka, who was always on the run, what was uppermost in her mind would be some man in Camp 55 or some woman in Camp 60 or some other unfortunate in Camp 63 who urgently needed her attention. How could she possibly take time off, even on the Sabbaths or holidays, when her family was suffering? When the camps closed she had more friends than anyone else in Israel. Rivka was loved by all.

Morris Laub bids farewell to Captain Ike at departure of the *Pan Crescent*.

Captain Ike

Captain Ike—or just Ike, as he was called by all who got to know him—had brought one of the Pan ships to Cyprus and had evidently taken the leading role in negotiations with the British. Ike turned out to be somewhat of a problem to us on the JDC staff and especially to Josh Leibner and me, with whom he was particularly at home. The problem was due to his frustration in trying to achieve his primary goal of bringing Jews to Palestine. Instead, here he was in Cyprus.

His two boats were under guard in Famagusta harbor. They could not be moved from port and he had all kinds of plans which were frustrated by the British. He wanted to steal the boats out in the dark of night. None of us understood how, but he was ready to try and had to be dissuaded. Then he wanted to blow up the boats, which, we feared, could easily be done. Frogmen were available and the necessary implements for explosion were also at hand. Ike was raring to go.

He simply could not abide sitting still. The seemingly interminable waiting, without being in the thick of the *Aliya Bet* battle against the British, was too much for him. It became one of my major tasks to keep an eye on Ike, to be a big brother to him and to remain in the area to cool him off. It all took too much of my time. I realized that something more drastic was necessary to curb Ike's intense desire to get off the island with the boats. I flew to Palestine and met with his superiors to convince them to do something to take Ike off my hands. I wanted to continue our relationship; I loved him and wanted him to be friendly with me, with my family and with our staff. I was taken by his exuberant personality, impressed by the tremendous experience this young man had already had, and by his love for Jews; but I could not adequately devote myself to keeping him from carrying out some of his designs which we all agreed would be disastrous for the cause in Cyprus. The *Mossad* people understood me and sent an emissary whose primary task was to be with Ike. It worked. I no longer had the main responsibility. Ike calmed down.

The boats had a store of supplies—food, linen, and other materials—which we needed on Cyprus. Though the *Aliya Bet* people and the JDC were engaged in the same task, the supplies nevertheless belonged to the former and so we negotiated business transactions, pure and simple. We bought the supplies from the *Pan Crescent* and they became part of our warehouse inventory.

A U.S. State Department Smear

Soon after the arrival of the Pan boats I received a cable from the writer I.F. Stone informing me that Secretary of State George Marshall had denounced the 15,000 passengers who had come to Cyprus on the boats as Communists and Communist agents, ostensibly because they came from Rumania, a Communist country.

I immediately got to work to try to discredit this smear. For one thing, I investigated the people and, apart from the 400 Bulgarians, I discovered via a questionnaire which the people filled out that one could not imagine a more bourgeois anti-Communist group. I wrote this up and sent it as a report to the JDC.

Moshe Pearlman was with us in Cyprus at the time. After talking about Stone's cable, we decided to go to Sir Godfrey Collins and, while talking to him about various matters, innocently slip in a question about the new arrivals. The idea was to get Sir Godfrey to say something contrary to the Marshall smear. Our scheme worked beyond our wildest expectations. When we asked Sir Godfrey whether he knew anything about the Pan arrivals, particularly about their "Communism", he said that he didn't think they were Communists, that he didn't know of any Communists; in essence, he denied the Marshall smear.

The Reuters correspondent at the time, a journalist by the name of Gibson Cowan, noted the story of Sir Godfrey's denial, which was spread throughout the newspapers in England and in the United States. The top British civil servant on Cyprus who was assigned to the camps, denied the allegations of the American Secretary of

40

State. We had scotched the Marshall story.

The Foreign Office wondered how it happened that Sir Godfrey did not know what Secretary of State Marshall had said. The only explanation I can come up with is that, even in the best of circumstances, even in the British Empire, slips do occur.

Reviewing *The New York Times* for that period, I learned that the British Foreign Office claimed that Sir Godfrey did not have the reports of security officers who had examined the new arrivals on the two ships. There were no such examinations. One of the points negotiated with the British by the captains of the Pan ships was that there would be no examinations. Only when this and other matters were agreed upon, did captains Ike and Gad turn their ships directly towards Cyprus rather than towards Palestine. The captains did not want any searches, not for the sake of communist agents whom they knew they were not transporting, but because they wanted to avoid the rough, often brutal, handling of the intercepted Jewish immigrants, and to prevent the occasional looting by British soldiers and sailors during the transfer to British naval vessels in Haifa. The agreement was carried out; there was no examination, either on the boats or upon landing in Famagusta. There was no investigation in the camps either.

The story does not end here. Washington, at least the State Department, was still convinced that thousands of Communists and Communist agents had arrived. Some months later a State Department official, Mr. Klass, came to Cyprus to see me. He was a Jew, spoke Hebrew, and seemed well aware of Jewish life in general and Palestinian life in particular and evidently had been sent to track down the truth. Who was right? Was Marshall or were we?

Klass and I went to lunch at the Four Lanterns restaurant in Larnaca. It lasted four hours. It was more than a lunch; I was grilled—a detailed investigation of life in the camps and a repeated attempt to get me to admit that thousands of Communists had come. Klass had with him pins which adherents of the various political parties in the camp wore. They were made from Cyprus coins right in the camp; they included *Hashomer Hatzair* pins and those of other leftist parties, and were inscribed with leftist slogans.

He confronted me with them and I explained what they were. At one point my temper, which I ordinarily tried to keep cool, got the better of me. I told him off. "You came to investigate me? You came to substantiate a falsehood? How could you? You who know so much about Jewish life and Jews in Israel—you who know what the *Hashomer Hatzair* is and any other of the kibbutz parties, left or right?"

Klass was not mollified. We left angry, he on his way to Palestine and I back to camp. I later learned that he wrote a long report to the State Department substantiating everything I said, and finally nailing the Marshall smear.

An Attempt to Blow Up a British Naval Vessel and an Escape

I have already stated that officially, even unofficially, I had as little to do with the *Haganah* as possible—with a few exceptions. One episode in which I openly played a part was the case of the Naval boat, the *Ocean Vigour*.

One morning during Passover of 1947 I learned in the camp that the *Ocean Vigour,* a British Naval vessel often used to transport intercepted Jewish immigrants from Haifa to Cyprus, was blown up while docked in a Famagusta port. It seems that a frogman, presumably from the camps, succeeded in planting a bomb underwater on the vessel, thereby disabling it. It was not destroyed, but it was damaged enough to have to remain in port for weeks until it could be repaired.

The police and the security forces were busily looking for the frogman. Apart from wondering about the incident and awaiting its outcome, there was nothing to do and I proceeded on my business as usual.

But that soon ended. I was informed that a young man from the camp (I will call him Etan) was found asleep on the beach. Etan was evidently exhausted from his swim to the *Ocean Vigour*. In trying to find his way to some shelter, he apparently dropped in sheer exhaustion, and was awakened by two men in uniform with guns pointed at him.

42

He was bustled off to the Famagusta jail and I was officially informed by the camp authorities and the Famagusta police. I immediately went to see him. He was not in a real jail, but rather in the Famagusta police station which had five or six cells attached. The police captain was a sympathetic elderly gentleman, who was friendly to me and acted decently toward Etan.

Etan and I spoke in Hebrew. I thought I recognized him as one of the internees and reminded him that, as it was a holiday, he could demand Passover food which would give him an opportunity to have somebody from the camp come every day to bring it. He readily agreed and when it was presented to the police and security authorities, they too agreed. One of the nurses in camp at the time was a young woman named Ruth Tenenbaum, who was asked to bring food and matzoh to Etan. One day during my almost daily visit, he told me he was bored and would like some books. I passed the word on and books were brought—Hebrew novels and other light works—which were inspected by the police and then given to him. Later, Etan told me he would like something weightier to read, a book of math for instance; word was passed on and a hard-cover trigonometry book in English was brought to him, together with the food, by Ruth Tenenbaum. In a day or two, he escaped. It seems that in the cover of the trigonometry book was a little saw or knife, so cleverly concealed that the book had passed muster by the police. Etan had used this knife to cut through the bars and had fled. He had left the book and the knife behind.

Ruth Tenenbaum was arrested as an accessory to his act. I was immediately informed of her arrest and was terribly perturbed; she was completely innocent; she had been used by the *Haganah*. I suppose the old saying that all is fair in love and war was true here. If the aim was to get Etan out of jail, anybody was fair game. I was distressed not only by her arrest but also by the fact that she was one of the JDC nurses. I felt that the JDC was seriously involved. I thereupon went to Prodromos Papavassiliou, a local Cypriot who owned a travel agency. From the very beginning we had used him as our agent for the purchase of air tickets, which became so frequent that, in time, his travel agency blossomed. He eventually became the Cyprus representative for El-Al and Zim. When I asked "Pap", as I called him, whether he could recommend an attorney for Ruth, he suggested Fuad Bey, a Turk by origin, the former Chief Justice of

43

the Cyprus Supreme Court and now a leading lawyer in private practice. That Pap, a Greek, had advised me to turn to a Turk was interesting to me. It illuminated the amicability between the two separate communities, the Greeks at that time representing 80% of the population and the Turks 20%. Although they inhabited different areas, nevertheless they had friendly relations. That was 1947; things have changed since.

I took Pap's advice and went to see Fuad Bey, a dignified, portly man of about 50 or 55, an Oxonian with a young son in school in England. He agreed to represent us and volunteered his usual fee; he would not take advantage of an American organization which was presumably rich.

Ruth was imprisoned in the gentlest way, under house arrest in the home of a police officer; she was given decent meals and a private room—rather nice, she told me—overlooking a garden. She was, however, terribly—and justifiably—agitated. The charge was serious and who knew what the consequences would be. Ruth was placed on trial about a week after the incident. During that period, the chief security officer went to Palestine to discuss the matter with his superiors in Jerusalem. Upon his return, the trial began. The charge was: aiding a prisoner to escape. I did not know the judge personally, but I saw him every day because he lived across the street from my house. I never knew he was a judge until I saw him in court. Though he was Greek, the trial was conducted in English because it was a British court. Yakobowski and I were called up and there was little that I could tell except that I had visited Etan and that Ruth Tenenbaum was a nurse in the employ of the JDC. However, I did upset the judge by refusing to take an oath on religious grounds. He adjourned the court and the next day agreed that I be permitted to affirm rather than swear.

The case against Ruth was open. She admitted that she brought the book; when she denied any knowledge of the knife, the prosecutor hammered away: it was she who brought the book and the knife and she was therefore an accessory to the escape. Fuad Bey presented an interesting and a strange defense. He claimed that Ruth was not an accessory at all, and couldn't be charged as being one because, though Etan was a prisoner, he had never actually been charged with any crime. It was true that he was arrested—but for what? He was held in jail by the police while he was waiting to

44

be charged. That being the case, said Fuad Bey, Ruth was absolved, and he asked that the case be dismissed.

The judge was apparently disturbed by this development, and adjourned the court to study the matter. A week later, he dismissed the case in recognition of Fuad Bey's defense. Ruth was placed on a plane and went home to Tel Aviv.

I was so intrigued that when I met Fuad Bey I asked him precisely what he had done. He said that he had based the case on a precedent established years earlier in a Common Court of England. He smiled, saying, "That's my profession. I looked through as many former cases as could possibly shed light and fortunately I came across this precedent." I thanked him for his work. When he presented his bill it was, I think, 50 or 100 pounds plus minimal expenses, and he said again, "I can't see myself charging you more than anyone else."

The story does not end here. Etan fled to an orange grove owned by Wilensky, a friendly Palestinian who helped the JDC in many ways and, as it turned out, was helpful to the *Haganah* in concealing persons waiting to escape.

From time to time, I would meet Fuad Bey for a drink or a cup of Turkish coffee. He told me that ever since the trial he had become *persona non grata* to the British and that he no longer attended a club whose membership was largely British. "Do you think this was anti-Semitism on their part?" I asked. "Yes, it is a little bit anti-Semitic," he said.

The police chief did not know that Etan had escaped to Palestine. After Etan's escape, whenever the monthly quota of internees was due to depart, the police chief would show up at the port, stand before every lorry, and scrutinize everyone descending to board the boat to Palestine. This futile search went on for months.

There was really just one victim in the whole incident—the elderly police captain—and we all felt very sorry for him. He was dismissed, I think even without entitlement to his pension. We asked that he be helped in ways that would not be known to the British; and the Palestinians as well as the JDC were able to help him.

Etan was later killed in battle in one of the Israeli-Arab wars.

46

Revolts in Camp

The internees, not knowing when they would be released, were on occasion rebellious. They were always eager to make their cause known in the hopes that Jews and others would assist in early release from their unjust incarceration and in the final closing of the camp.

The Demonstration at the Gates of Camp 55

Camp 55 was the first of the Caraolos camps to which deportees were brought. Though everything possible was being done by the JDC to help relieve the endless wait, what we did was not enough for the internees to become quiet. They were prisoners. They knew and we knew that they were unjustly held. They had every right to make their feelings known.

One day a group assembled at the gates and demanded their release. The group grew and soon the demands turned into a snide, almost raucous berating of the British and their policy and finally into insistence on the opening of the camp. The British security section of the Army came, stood outside the gates, confronted the internees, and warned them to disperse and go back to their tents. They refused. The warning was repeated; the refusal stuck. The man in charge of the security section was a foppish major, the very carica-ture of a British Army man, the veritable distortion of Colonel Blimp. It was this major who ordered the dispersal; when the internees remained adamant, he ordered his men to shoot. They shot and Shlomoh Chaimson, one of the persons at the very front, was killed. This act, so unlike the behavior of the British in the camps, was a tremendous shock not only to the internees but also to Major Newman and his subordinates who worked inside the camps and had contact with the internees. They never expressed their shock to me, but it was obvious from their demeanor and their sense of humiliation. Shlomoh Chaimson's death was the cause of more demonstrations, but this time inside the camp, and when he was brought out on the shoulders of his comrades to the lorry that took him to his resting place in Margoa Cemetery, Major Newman stood at attention in silent tribute.

The Hunger Strike

All our efforts to increase the quotas and to close the camps were in vain and, except for a very rare relaxation such as that afforded to Rabbi Isaac Semiatitzky of London, the 750 monthly quota stood firmly. The agony of waiting kept mounting. One day someone in the Central Committee conceived the idea of a hunger strike for the entire camp, with the possible exception of pregnant women and nursing mothers. The matter was discussed repeatedly in the Central Committee, among the emissaries, and with the JDC staff, and a hunger strike was declared. The world soon knew about it. The news appeared everywhere, especially in the Palestinian press. The strike went on for four or five days and then was called off. It was so effective that the leaders of the *Yishuv* (Palestine Jewish Community) cabled us to end it and promised increased endeavors to get the camps closed. Similar appeals were made to the internees, who finally agreed to stop the strike because of the ravages caused by hunger. The internees acceded to these many appeals.

I suppose the time has come to tell the true story of the strike. It was a hoax. There never really was a hunger strike. In preparation for an apparent strike, supplies were stored in warehouses in the camp and distributed quietly from day to day, concealed from the British watchtower guards. The amount of food was diminished and the internees received less than usual—but it was not a hunger strike. However, the situation seemed critical even to the leaders of Palestine; their reaction was proof that they were taken in. It is hard for me to assess whether it had an effect on any of Bevin's policy decisions. I would like to believe that it did. But Bevin was a hard man, stubborn and difficult to cross. The strike did influence world opinion and was thereby effective if that had any role in Bevin's final decision to close the camps.

The Demolishing of the JDC Staff Room in Dekhelia

The JDC workers, staff, emissaries, and anybody else associated with us lived in camp, except for very few persons such as Leibner, Yacobi, and later one or two of the doctors. There was daily work with the internees in camp and the workers ate there, slept there, and tried to find there whatever recreation they could; but once in a while they would go out of camp for a break. Most of the time, however, they stayed in camp, and in recognition of this fact, we outfitted one of the Nissen huts in Dekhelia as a JDC staff room. There, one could have a smoke, a cup of tea, read a newspaper, chat, take a rest, and insofar as was possible, be away from the hurly-burly of work for at least a moment. The staff room was outfitted a little differently from most of the huts in the camps and was primarily reserved for the staff—though now and then a member of the Central Committee would come in. It must have aroused some resentment, and perhaps jealousy; certainly there were exaggerated notions about the special treatment accorded the JDC staff. The staff's salary was very low, and the work was virtually 24 hours a day, 7 days a week—the kind of work done only by persons imbued with devotion. Various accounts of life in the ghetto indicate that the very nature of the ghetto brought out total commitment on the part of leaders and those on the road to leadership. It was the same kind of process in Cyprus. Nevertheless, internees' resentment of their incarceration and their inability to influence the British turned by projection into hostility toward the JDC.

The hostility mounted until one day a band invaded the staff room in Dekhelia and wrecked it. I immediately determined a course of action and called the JDC staff to a meeting: I was going to pull the entire JDC out of the camps until an apology came from the internees. They had to understand that we were not the British. My staff left the camps: doctors, lawyers, educators, nurses, and warehouse workers; and much to my surprise and satisfaction, the emissaries also left. I sent word to the internees that if that's what they thought of the JDC, it would be well if we left and they got along with what the British would provide. The removal of medical attention was particuarly irksome to us and certainly harmful to the internees.

Naturally I informed the JDC in New York and in Paris of what was going on, and their reply was that I was on the scene and it was up to me to do as I saw fit. I was determined to stay out until an apology came and I marvel that I was able to hold fast to my determination. It was out of character for me but I felt that an important principle was at stake and that it had to be established—or re-established: that the JDC was a voluntary organization, sent by Americans and Palestinians, staffed by Americans and Palestinians, financed by American Jewish money, with one aim—to alleviate the suffering and the boredom on Cyprus and to convert the enforced stay into a period of usefulness. We were not going to go back until this principle was recognized. After a day or so some of my staff became troubled and asked me to rethink my order. I refused. Rabbi Ehrenbourg, one of the rabbis working with the *Agudas Israel*, came to see my wife Eve, and pleaded with her to intervene with me and call off our absence. Eve correctly said that she did not participate in such matters; she would inform me of the rabbi's plea, but would in no way take any stand herself.

Finally, after three or four days, word came that there was a change of heart among the internees. I went in with only David Landwehr (now Landor), who was the deputy in the winter camps. I addressed the assembled campers in Yiddish. It was a long speech that I made—maybe two hours—but neither oratorical nor admonitory. I simply recited what the JDC was doing for them and ended with the statement that their apology was accepted and that we would come back. I learned from that experience that we took our work too much for granted. We did everything, but did not inform the people what we were doing. Public relations even inside the camp were important and, henceforth, we made sure that the people in camp, not just the Central Committee, knew about our role.

These three revolts: the gates of Camp 55, the "hunger strike", and the rebellion against the JDC, were expressions of protest—attempts to cry out to the world for help. All through their stay, there was among the internees an underlying feeling that injustice was being perpetrated against them and a mounting resentment against the causes of that injustice. And it should not have been otherwise; even the revolt against the JDC I came to see in that spirit and to perceive it as an expression of that resentment.

The *Youth Aliya* on Cyprus

The *Youth Aliya*, the fabled Jewish organization established by Henrietta Szold for the rescue and education of orphaned and otherwise unattached youth in Israel, naturally became interested in Cyprus. When the Cyprus camps were thought to be a temporary situation, the *Youth Aliya* anticipated working with the internees when they arrived in Palestine. But as soon as it became established that the internment camps were there to stay for a long time, the *Youth Aliya* decided to come to Cyprus.

Its director at that time was Hans Beit, who flew over to Famagusta early in 1947 to talk to me and look at the camps. He thought the matter over and then made the following proposals: He would like to have a team of *Youth Aliya's* top workers come over to Cyprus to work with the youth who needed its kind of expertise; to use its rehabilitation services—especially for those who had been hurt psychologically by the vicissitudes of the war, the concentration camps, the DP camps, and now the internment camps on Cyprus.

He envisioned gathering together such youth in a part of the camp which would be supervised by *Youth Aliya* personnel acting in cooperation with their own medical team, members of staff and emissaries who could be of service. The idea sounded good, and I agreed.

Soon after Beit's visit, the first group of *Youth Aliya* people came. Among others they included Chanoh Reinhold (now Rinot), a leading educator who formerly held major positions in the Ministry of Education; Akiba Vanchotzker, the Director of the famous *Youth Aliya* village, Ben Shemen; and Dr. Rappaport, the psychology specialist.

After a survey of the camp, conferences with the Committee and

51

the emissaries, and discussions with me, we decided to bring together children and unattached youth (though occasionally a boy or girl who had parents in the camp was included), to have them undergo special treatment and prepare them for their future in Palestine; if they were young enough they would be involved in regular *Youth Aliya* organizations, if older, they would join one of the kibbutzim.

Reinhold, Vanchotzker, Rappaport and their colleagues threw themselves into the work with an extraordinary degree of determination and vigor. Like all of us, they were motivated by the sheer presence of Jewry on the threshold of Palestine, and by the needs that had to be met, especially of the young people who could perhaps be helped more than others.

Education and Culture

Life in the camps was not limited to supplying bodily needs and medical care. Spiritual needs also had to be taken into account. They were supplied by the internees, who were helped by emissaries, teachers, and cultural workers.

Not only did the children have to be educated, but the adults as well. There were many reasons for adult education: time was heavy on their hands; the schooling of most adults had been interrupted by war, life in the ghettoes, and the struggle to survive; Palestine was accessible at last, even if preceeded by a stay behind barbed wire, and Hebrew and Jewish culture had to be learned.

To fill this need, theatre groups, choirs, and dance groups were organized by the internees. The acting, singing, or dancing may have lacked professional polish but the spirit affirmed the declaration from the Psalms, *I shall not die but shall live.*

The language in the camps was largely Yiddish. One could also hear European languages and even Arabic. Practically everyone tried to study Hebrew. Central Committee meetings and minutes were in Yiddish as were the exchanges the internees had with me and other JDC workers.

Athletics and sports groups (mainly soccer) also existed and competed with one another. The meager supplies, provided by the movements and the JDC, had to be carefully guarded. Because there was time to play, many more played than would have in everyday life; one could always see or participate in a game.

The Rutenberg Foundation

The Rutenberg Foundation of Haifa had a primary purpose— adult education. Baruch Rubinstein was the director during the years when I was in Cyprus and for many years after.

He came to the camps and brought over teachers, mimeograph machines and useful paraphernalia to help introduce and augment a

Dramatic production by the Dekhelia camp theatre group.

Above: Art exhibition at Caraolos camp.

Right: Scene from a Dekhelia camp theatre production.

Scene from Sholom Aleichem's "Mazal Tov" presented by the Caraolos Dramatic Group.

cultural program among adults. Of medium height, about 40 when he arrived, he was a man of few words, full of zeal and new ideas for easing life as it was known on Cyprus. A member of the Rubinstein family of cosmetic fame, he visited rather often and every visit resulted in something new in the area of culture—perhaps a daily paper or a textbook for a particular camp. His projects were generally funded by the Foundation and occasionally in joint partnership with the JDC, always with our consultation and approval.

I often met him after Cyprus; while his Rutenberg Foundation went on to carry out its aims, Cyprus was the acme of its activities.

The Rutenberg Seminar

In Haifa there was an institute for cultural workers organized and named after the Rutenberg Foundation. In July, 1947, after negotiations and a visit to the camps by executive director Baruch Rubinstein, the Rutenberg Seminar was opened. There were not only seminars, but lectures, art classes, and other cultural activities. The Rutenberg Foundation found the teachers, acquired the books for a library, and financed 40% of the budget. The JDC provided 50% of the budget, and the youth department of the Zionist Organization the remaining 10%. When the War of Independence broke out in May, 1948, the JDC began covering the entire budget for the seminar, which was changed to the "JDC Rutenberg Seminar."

The Seminar was unique in many ways. Its language was Hebrew and its program non-partisan. The activities were varied; its curricula were strict, and its teachers selected for their pedagogic skills and cultural attainments. Today many of the 27 teachers involved are leading professors at the Hebrew University and elsewhere. About 1,800 persons studied at the Seminar; many of its alumni went into teaching and others have pursued higher studies. The courses were designed for beginners, advanced students and "teachers." About a third of the students had completed elementary school or had studied in a *cheder* and a few had university or yeshiva training. The formal studies, demanding several hours a day, were devoted to Hebrew, Bible, Palestine, Jewish history, Zionism, and the Jewish community of Palestine. Each student spent four to six weeks in formal study.

But the Seminar did not confine itself to formal studies. Every weekend lecturers were brought over from Palestine to talk at the "people's" university and teach short but intensive courses. In addition, actors and singers came to show their solidarity with their brothers and sisters in the camps. Between July, 1948 and January, 1949, the Seminar issued a mimeographed Hebrew weekly newspaper completely written by students and alumni. Its libraries had over 4,000 books which were eagerly read.

The art department also deserves mention. Naftali Bezem, now an internationally acclaimed artist, and his students devoted themselves to painting, printing and engraving. A book of linocuts was issued by them in turn. After Bezem left, his place was taken by Zeev Ben-Zvi, the famous Palestine sculptor, who organized and led a sculpture class attended by many who had never held a chisel or fingered clay. My son Levi, at age ten, attended the sculpture class and I still have a piece of his sculpture. Photographs of many of these sculptures were later taken and assembled into an album.

All in all the Rutenberg Seminar and its teachers labored far beyond the call of duty.

Vocational Training

To eat, study, play, sing, dance, or act does not fill one's day. How to make time productive remained a problem.

The problem of work concerned all of us. Not only was valuable time lost in waiting, but the honing of skills already acquired and the acquisition of new ones were victims of enforced idleness.

When I brought this problem to the attention of the authorities and suggested the JDC be permitted to set up workshops, the answer was "No." The reason given was that workshops meant acquiring tools which could be used to cut barbed wire and facilitate escapes. I did not accept this answer and made myself obnoxious and persistent in asking. I used every opportunity to do so, sparing no one in Cyprus, Jerusalem, Cairo (the seat of the British Middle East Headquarters), or London. I asked our visitors to the camps to intervene—which they gladly did—but no workshops were permitted. Suddenly, after more than a year of waiting and prodding, permission was granted.

56

The JDC brought in tools and even some machinery. Many internees knew a little tailoring or cobbling and other miscellaneous trades. Workshops were set up to teach wiring, tailoring, cobbling and carpentry among other skills. The teachers were usually internees themselves, and some emissaries were brought in to teach, supervise, and administer. The *Histadrut* and other groups in Palestine cooperated, all contributing to make the workshops a success.

Some who had to stay in the camps for a long time learned a new trade or perfected an old one. Those who stayed for a shorter period also did useful work. Time was no longer a master, but became a slave.

Were the British right in their contention that the tools would be used to cut wire? No and yes. For most, the workshops served a legitimate purpose. A very few used the tools to cut wire and escapes took place. So what?

Children, Children, and More Children

My interest in children and their education, (I had been a teacher for over eighteen years before joining the JDC) was heightened during the Second World War. We knew that the Nazis had hunted and killed children as well as adults (we know now that a million Jewish children were exterminated) and that schools and the usual educational processes were disrupted. This predicament is what I was faced with upon my arrival in Cyprus.

The same problems confronted others as well, including Moshe Yaari, a functionary of *Youth Aliya*. He arrived from Jerusalem in November, 1946, in order to prepare a program of *aliya* for the young. Yaari was serving as the emissary of the Jewish Agency and could not devote his full time to educational problems. Nevertheless, he did worry about the children and tried to find out as much as he could about them. Thus we learn from his January 1947 report that the camps had about 1,000 children, many of them orphans who were under the sponsorship of various political parties. Of 585 children that came on the *Knesset Israel* (585 out of 3,845 passengers) 77% or 450 were orphans. In December 1946, Camp 64, the so-called winter camp at Xylotymbu, was opened, and most of the children were concentrated there. Not all the children had moved on to the Kfar Noar (youth village, as Camp 64 came to be called) under *Youth Aliya* sponsorship, and for these children educational matters were still haphazardly though conscientiously handled by the parties. A change took place in January 1947, soon after the arrival of Chanoch Reinhold (now Dr. Rinot), a leader of stature in the *Youth Aliya* of Jerusalem. He labored long and hard to give the children an adequate education, to give them proper goals in life, and to prepare them for Palestine. He converted the children's village into an educational workshop.

At that time the children's village represented the greatest collection of Jewish children in any one place in the world. Its population kept growing as more boatloads of Jews heading for Palestine were deported to Cyprus. Reinhold was able to report that, on June 29, 1947, there were 1,775 children and youth, 985 of them orphans. In the same report, Reinhold says that 43% were from Poland, 32% from Hungary, 13% from Rumania, 7% from Czechoslovakia, and 5% from other countries. Because of their number, the children's village had to expand to other areas of the Xylotymbu camps.

Because the parties maintained an important role in the youth village, although less pervasive than before Reinhold's arrival, the class structure was based on the parties rather than on age. Sometimes a class would have children whose ages spanned six or seven years. For many of the children, the party became mother, father, and the goal in life. The parties did not want to lose their children through an overall mixture, but in general they did cooperate with each other. The "teachers" who came with the children were largely untrained, but imbued with their idealistic love for the children, the party, and Palestine. The children had been in hiding with the teachers, in forests, in partisan groups, and the teachers knew the children best—their ability to survive as well as their shortcomings. These presented special character problems which could not be overcome easily. A child who saw plunder, theft, cruelty, and death could not suddenly shed some of his survival techniques upon coming to Cyprus; for did they not have to use them even at Haifa, when they were transferred from their boats to British naval vessels for deportation to the camps at Cyprus? Was it not legitimate to "organize" (a polite word for steal) things that belonged to someone else, (especially if he or she were a member of another party group) or to steal things from the JDC? To divest the children of these acquired habits was painful. Reinhold and those in charge grasped this matter—altogether the children's village had 36 trained emissaries from the *Aliyat Hanoar* in Palestine. They did not stay all the time between January 1947 and May 1948 when *Aliyat Hanoar* functioned on Cyprus, because the work was arduous and emotionally taxing: that is why the turnover was great. Reinhold did stay longer than most, about half a year, and he regarded his task, though particularly demanding, as extremely rewarding. He felt that he and his colleagues were doing holy work. The *Youth Aliya* emissaries did not only have to school the children, but also to give guidance to the internee teachers as much as possible. There were about 150 of them, mostly non-professional, when the children's village population was at its peak. The curriculum was stern, yet adapted to the special needs of the children. The study of Hebrew, information concerning Palestine, and arithmetic took 22 hours a week. Advanced students also studied the Bible, history, general geography, and some even studied natural science. In the classes of the *B'nai Akiva* (orthodox children who came from the *Mizrachi*), twelve hours a week were devoted to "sacred" studies. There was even a *B'nai Akiva yeshivah*, where about 30 youths spent 5 hours daily on sacred studies and 5 hours daily on non-sacred studies.

This was not all. The *Youth Aliya* was in charge of all of a child's time, 168 hours a week. Aside from eating, sleeping, and doing homework, the children had a lot of free time and a variety of motivations: that is why weekends were very important. Friday evenings became longed-for events and everyone looked forward to them: although their clothes were shabby, they all wore at least clean shirts. The holidays became focal points when many of the non-formal traits of decent cooperation, planned programming and talk about the final goal, Palestine, were foremost. Songs and dances heightened these events—altogether a therapeutic and welcome change from the drudgery and oppressiveness of daily camp life.

In addition to the usual festivities, there were special party celebrations including May Day. Since most parties were affiliated with the *Histadrut*, May Day played a large role for which preparations went on for weeks. On the eve of May 1st, about 1,500 children gathered in a kind of amphitheater to participate in and observe a gigantic torchlight parade. Similarly, *Tu Beshvat*, Jewish Arbor Day, was celebrated widely, even with symbolic planting of trees.

Also *Betar*, the youth movement of the Zionist Revisionists, had its adherents on Cyprus. As was customary they drilled and marched with flags and slogans that enraged the other parties. Occasional fisticuffs and other acts of violence broke out between *Betar* and *Histadrut* adherents, leading to an attempt to keep *Betar* out of the *Youth Aliya* hegemony. However, Jerusalem headquarters decided otherwise and Betar was allowed in.

To be part of *Youth Aliya* was important not only because of the educational advantages, but also because *Youth Aliya* children, namely, those registered in the children's village, received extra rations. In March 1947, I participated in a meeting in Jerusalem which laid down the ground rules for *Youth Aliya* and JDC coopera- tion. We agreed that the JDC would help finance the educational needs such as classroom furniture, classroom materials including books, pencils and notebooks (the Palestine Committee for the Cyprus exiles undertook to supply basic needs, but because of its limited funds the JDC agreed to supplement these supplies on a fifty-fifty basis), and to give each child, aged 4 to 16, supplemental food: oranges, tomatoes, jam, cocoa, powdered milk, vegetables, lemon juice, fats, and bread. The supplement added up to 600 calories daily and was in addition to the normal JDC supplement available to all internees and to the usual adult ration of about 2,100 calories supplied by the British authorities.

Another advantage of being part of the *Youth Aliya* was participa- tion in its innovative camp-within-a-camp, a kind of "special summer camp" for children of all ages. The usual camp activities went on, but the 50 children or so gathered in it were on "vacation" to improve themselves, physically and psychologically. Clean white sheets, a rarity, were provided for all; learning in a particularly quiet atmos- phere was paramount; play was designed with character goals in mind, and there was more food. The children ate five times a day, including morning and afternoon snacks, totalling 3,800 calories daily. The additional number of calories was supplied by the JDC, and to a minor degree by the British. The camp within the camp was successful, the children gained weight, they studied, they played, and they forgot, insofar as possible behind barbed wire, the past and the present, and focused on the future.

Kindergarten at Camp Caraolos (author's son Marc, bottom photo, third from left).

Children Not Under Youth Aliya Sponsorship

As already indicated, not all children were under *Youth Aliya* sponsorship. Besides, there remained some children even after *Youth Aliya* was officially liquidated in the middle of the year 1948. *Youth Aliya* was in charge of all orphans and of many children with one or two parents, though educating children whose parents were with them was a departure from *Youth Aliya*'s principles, since it was an organization which worked in schools, farms, kibbutzim, and moshavim, especially with orphans. Yet there were always children, orphans as well as others fortunate enough to have parents, who were not under *Youth Aliya* control and who had to be provided for educationally.

When the children's village opened up in the Xylotymbu camp at the end of 1946, about 250 children and youths remained at Caraolos. They had no party affiliation or else belonged to the *Noar Zioni*, a movement that was worried lest its youthful adherents be swallowed up by the various *Histadrut* parties that kept functioning in the youth village. The village and the parties looked after these children, but their educational work was deficient. True, the JDC helped with books and other materials and with additional food, but that was not enough. Although the schools were filled with eager pupils and enthusiastic "teachers," what was lacking was coordination and guidance. These were luckily supplied by the Rutenberg Foundation of Haifa which, after a visit by its energetic executive director, Baruch Rubinstein, jumped into the vacuum. The Foundation devoted itself to all the cultural needs of the camps and catered to children as well as adults. It sent teachers and other emissaries, among them Shmaryahu Zalmanowitz (now Professor Talmon of the Hebrew University). While still working under the *Youth Aliya* sponsorship Zalmanowitz proved to be such an imaginative leader and so devoted to the cause, that when the *Youth Aliya* left, the JDC asked him to supervise all of the schools. In January 1947, besides kindergartens and nursery schools in Caraolos, there were two small party schools alongside the *Aliyat No Hanoar* in Xylotymbu: that of Mapai and that of the *Agudas Israel*. The number of pupils grew so fast that there were approximately 360 children in Caraolos alone when the camps closed. The studies were generally extensive, strict, motivating, and were all conducted in Hebrew. A special feature of the schools was the period between 6 A.M. and 8 A.M. when its non-professional teachers gathered for intensive self-study and courses given by the trained teachers brought over by the Rutenberg Foundation.

Barbed wire notwithstanding, the children in the Cyprus camps were not neglected. Despite obstacles, the traditional drive for education overcame the laziness and despair to which it was so easy to succumb. No one obliged the children to attend school, yet all came. Truancy was rare. *Davka* (an often-used word meaning "despite it all"), motivation and the lure of Palestine combined to make even an internment camp a place in which school was vital.

The First Director of Culture and the Poet Nathan Alterman

Zeev Chernasky, also known as Zeev Aaron, was the cultural activist in Cyprus upon my arrival. A famous poet, editor of a children's journal, and the cultural supervisor of the *Haganah*, he came to Cyprus at his own request and remained there for months to help "people of the book" remain true to their nature even when under guard.

About 50 years old when I met him, he was warm and down-to-earth with a certain charisma which attracted everybody. He had traveled a good deal in America and other countries, and I was delighted to know him. Zeev was also glad to meet me, glad that I knew Hebrew and that I had some awareness of Jewish cultural activities.

Zeev left physical matters to others; his primary concern was the spirit, though he obviously did not separate physical needs from the spiritual. Was it Rabbi Israel Salanter who once said, "Another man's physical needs are my spiritual needs?" Zeev acted in accordance with this perceptive observation.

Zeev and I walked around the camps very often. He spoke Yiddish to the internees, while he conversed in Hebrew. I recall making an impression on him purely by accident, certainly not by design, when I was distressed to hear some internees greet me as "Herr Direktor." I repeatedly told them my name was Moishe Laub, and that I was not their director or anyone else's. It took a long time before the message got across. Zeev helped me.

He brought over some teachers—some of whom he selected and all of them good—and they remained in camp for a few months, some for longer periods.

After Zeev left, I visited him in Tel Aviv. I used to go to Palestine at least once every three months and of course I had to see Zeev at the first opportunity. He took me to the famous Café Kassit, the gathering place of Tel Aviv's literati, and pointed out to me writers, poets, novelists, essayists, old, young, some famous and some who hoped to become famous. He showed me a big, fat volume, saying "I suppose there's no other café in the world where you will find this volume." It was Mandelkern's Hebrew concordance to the Bible. It was obviously often used to settle disputes about words, their origin, their usage, etc.

Zeev pointed to a table where a man in his forties was surrounded by a coterie; he spoke boisterously, greeting everyone near him. Zeev asked me whether I had ever heard of Nathan Alterman. I was familiar with some of his poetry, and once in a while, when I did get the Cyprus camps' newspaper, the *Davar*, I would read in it his famous "Tur Shvi'i" or "Seventh Column," which was a remarkable review of the news of the week in verse, often resulting in sheer poetry. "Alterman was on his way to being real drunk," Zeev said, "and probably soon you'll see him stagger out. He may even reel in to the gutters, but don't be concerned. He'll find his way home. Everybody knows that he drinks, but that in no way stops him from writing great poetry."

Later Nathan Alterman came to Cyprus and, knowing his habits, I stocked my bar with good Cyprus wines and Cognac, ready for the great visitor. But in Cyprus, where he stayed for three days, he refused to accept a drink and remained sober throughout his visit. I imagine that he could not get himself to indulge in his habits in the midst of the terrible misery that surrounded us.

He walked through the camps, observing everything with a concerned expression. He addressed one or two groups and his remarks, couched in beautiful Yiddish or Hebrew, were a combination of depression and ultimate hope. When he left he embraced me and wept and then sent me one of his books, a collection of his Seventh Column, as a memento of his visit.

He wrote about Cyprus, but upon his return to Tel Aviv, Alterman went back to the Café Kassit and to his usual life style.

Other Cultural Workers

One of the teachers whom Baruch Rubinstein brought over was Dov Newman. He could teach anything having to do with Judaic studies, and could do it in Hebrew or in Yiddish. He was also willing to resort to any means to further his teaching, such as using slides or mimeographed materials. Teaching to him did not mean merely classroom activity. Teaching encompassed life, so it meant making a newspaper possible, lending new interest to meetings, organizing choruses, helping in celebrations, furthering dramatic activities, in other words, doing anything that would bring the air of Palestine to the camp itself and that would make the internees more easily adjustable to Palestine.

Dov Newman, who was a Rutenberg Seminar teacher and is now Professor Noy of the Hebrew University and a folklore specialist of international repute, had a brother who was an internee in camp named Meier Newman. Meier was a musician, composer, and chorus master, and Dov and Meier conceived the idea of producing a "Cyprus Songster," "Shiron Kabbriein," which included various well-known melodies as well as melodies written inside the camps. The songster is now a rarity and he who possesses it indeed possesses a treasure. Meier Noy is a teacher and composer in Tel Aviv, and has gathered and catalogued the finest collection in the entire world of Yiddish and Hebrew songs. He lives in a modest apartment and is totally immersed in his work as a music teacher in the public schools of Tel Aviv and as the collector and cataloguer of this unique musical archive. It is to be hoped that some day it will be preserved in one of the great universities of Israel where it belongs.

It was a strange coincidence that the two brothers, who had not seen each other for many years, should meet in Cyprus, one free to go and come as he wished and the other interned behind the barbed wire. I had a cousin among the internees whom I would visit occasionally and bring gifts, but he was never treated differently from the other internees because he was a member of my family. He now lives and thrives in the city of Beer Sheva.

Artists and Other Celebrities

Among the internees were men and women of fame in the countries from which they came. Let me mention only three examples. Shraga Weill, now a world-famous Israeli artist, was still a young man while on Cyprus, but already an artist of talent who kept on working during the months of his internment. Upon his arrival in Palestine, he became well-known as an illustrator of books and as a painter.

The late Izhak Paner was a great Yiddish writer. He wrote about Cyprus later, after arriving in Palestine, and was a steady contributor to the *Goldene Keit,* (the *Golden Link*,) the best quarterly in the world devoted to Yiddish literature, now in its fourth decade.

Dr. Wishnizer was a surgeon who came on the Pan ships and, because of the special need for surgery during the wars, he was given priority by the Central Committee to leave. He died a few years ago; his work, like that of other doctors, was of tremendous importance to the people of Palestine.

The internment in Cyprus made no distinctions. Everybody who was caught in the net of the British was deported. But the internees recognized whom they had in their midst and honored them as they deserved.

My Meetings with Ben-Gurion and with Bernadotte and Bunche

As the camp population grew, the need for staff and emissaries grew as well. The JDC was able to fill the former pretty quickly, but the number of the latter was inadequate. While I was not directly concerned with the emissaries, I nevertheless recognized their value to the internees and was impressed with their work. They were technically members of the JDC staff.

Despite numerous appeals from the various party groups that more emissaries be sent to Cyprus, not enough of them came. In desperation, Moshe Brachman of the Committee for the Cyprus Exiles, a Palestine committee helping the internees, suggested that I go and see David Ben-Gurion about this matter.

After a few weeks, I was notified by Mr. Brachman that Ben-Gurion was ready to see me. His office in Tel Aviv was in a heavily guarded building on Yarkon Street, then, as now, a street with many hotels. I was told that Ben-Gurion would allot 15 minutes to my interview so I had to concentrate all my requests within that time. When I was ushered into his office, I saw that Ben-Gurion looked exactly like in the photographs: an imposing man with a face to remember, recognizably a leader at first glimpse.

He listened to me practically without interruption, occasionally asking a question. As I talked he jotted notes in a little black book. We talked about conditions in Cyprus, the state of mind of the internees, the attitude of the British. The meeting lasted more than an hour-and-a-half.

I assumed that Ben-Gurion was impressed with the situation as I presented it. My assumption was correct. Soon after the meeting, emissary after emissary began to arrive and the scarcity of emissaries was no longer the theme of the day.

My meeting with Ben-Gurion is one of the events of my stay on Cyprus that is most impressed in my memory. I will never forget his quiet, intent attention and his little notebook. Later I was told that the black notebook always accompanied him and was not only a record of events and people he met but also furnished him with the raw material for his essays and speeches.

Bernadotte and Bunche

When Israel came into being on May 15, 1948, the Arabs attacked and Israel found itself at war with its surrounding neighbors. Attempts were made at finding a way out as quickly as possible and finally Count Folke Bernadotte of Sweden was able to achieve a cease fire under the aegis of the United Nations. The first one was broken, but another one was finally arranged at Bernadotte's insistence. Bernadotte was able to get both parties in the conflict to sit down with him at a neutral place and discuss peace terms. The place was Rhodes, one of the Dodecanese Islands, now back under the sovereignty of Greece, after being under Italy's rule between World War I and World War II.

The terms of the cease fire included a clause that made it difficult for new forces, even within the respective boundaries, to be added to already existing armies. Insofar as the people of Cyprus were concerned, this meant that no one would be allowed to go to Palestine (now Israel) during the cease fire and that all people were to stay until peace was finally achieved. The people of the camp became increasingly restless. The rise of the State of Israel added to their eagerness to leave. They felt particularly aggrieved at being hostages on Cyprus, when at last a Jewish state existed and they could be of help. We of the staff, the JDC, and the *Haganah* were equally restless.

It occurred to us that it might be a good idea for me to go to see Bernadotte in Rhodes and ask him to release internees on humanitarian grounds. The cease fire found many families torn asunder. Some members of a family had left on earlier boats, while others were left in Cyprus. This was cruel. An appeal to Bernadotte might help. Of course, I agreed to go, but since Rhodes was now a part of Greece and there were no direct flights from Cyprus to Rhodes, I had to go to Athens first. Before leaving, I sent a wire to Ruben Zaslanyi, chief negotiator for the Israelis in Rhodes, asking his opinion about whether my intervention was desirable. He cabled, "Yes, come as quickly as you can. Bernadotte awaits you." I went to Athens, applied for a visa which was soon granted with the help of the JDC. The JDC had now a permanent office in Athens, a far cry from the set-up that existed in the spring of 1945 when I worked there for the UN Relief and Rehabilitation Administration by day and for the JDC in the evenings and during my free hours. I cabled Zaslanyi that I was coming and flew on to Rhodes.

Rhodes is a beautiful island, with bougainvilleas blossoming everywhere. The famous Colossus of Rhodes is one of the seven wonders of the world. The Colossus no longer exists, but Rhodes still is a wonder of the world because of its natural beauty and the way the medieval character of the the city has been preserved. The Knights of St. John had their seat in Rhodes during the tenth century, and that portion of the city in which they dwelled remains as it was hundreds of years ago. It is, of course, interesting to the historian and an aesthetic joy to the beholder. The more recent history of Rhodes includes a particularly Jewish facet, namely, that Mussolini had established a Hebraic seminary on the island which in due course made it possible to educate rabbis who took their places as Sephardic leaders in various Jewish communities.

The peace negotiations took place in the Hotel Des Roses, a luxurious establishment on the beach, at this time empty of all visitors except for the negotiators who occupied all the rooms. I announced my presence to Count Bernadotte and was told to see him in his suite the next morning at 8 A.M. I was surprised to find another person there, Ralph Bunche. Both were in pajamas having breakfast. I accepted coffee and quickly explained the problems. Both men listened intently. However, I sensed a difference in their reaction. The Count seemed sympathetic, but Bunche appeared skeptical. I was told I would get an answer the next day and was given an appointment to meet them, of all places, on the beach, at 4 o'clock in the afternoon. Between breakfast that day and the next afternoon, I walked around Rhodes, enjoyed the sights and dropped into a movie. I sat in the balcony and near me sat a friendly woman and her children. They spoke Swedish and I correctly guessed they were members of Bernadotte's family; in fact, they were his wife and children. They were very kind; they talked to me as if they had known me for some time, though they didn't know who I was. I was struck by the unassuming, democratic approach of this family to a stranger. The next day I counted the minutes until 4 o'clock. They dragged on because of my anxiety. I went to the beach and there were Bernadotte, Bunche and others, swimming. It was a hot day, a good day to take a swim. I sat down on the beach and they spotted me and came over. Bernadotte asked me some questions and, upon my assurance that this would be a family reunion matter only, he more or less agreed. I say "more or less" because Ralph Bunche was in the way. He kept reminding Bernadotte of the terms of the truce, warned him that he might be alienating the Arabs if he acceded to my requests, that it would jeopardize the peace talks; altogether, Bunche didn't think it was a good idea. I thanked the Count for his

70

understanding and hoped that we would hear a positive answer from him soon. Bernadotte asked me how I was going back and I replied that I had to wait a few days for a commercial plane; he kindly put at my disposal his own plane which brought me directly back to Cyprus. Within a few days, sure enough, word came that Bernadotte had agreed to my request, and 500 people were allowed to rejoin their families.

Now this can be told: this reunion of families was fiction. What were needed were fighters and the 500 who left were young people who could quickly be taken into the Israeli Army. They were indeed quickly enlisted and fought in the battle of Latrun; to my horror, most of them lost their lives. This tragedy has weighed heavily on my conscience all these years. I felt responsible and in a way I still feel responsible for their death; yet, at the time, I was convinced that it was the correct thing to get fighters over to Israel as quickly as possible.

Bernadotte was assassinated and Ralph Bunche took over. Bunche, by his wisdom, shrewdness, honesty, and perseverance was able to bring about the peace, and he deservedly received the Nobel Prize. The Bunche who carried on the negotiations after Bernadotte's assassination seemed to be a different man from the Bunche I had met in his pajamas and later on the beach with Bernadotte. Sometimes later in discussing this with Moses Beckelman, then Director General for Overseas Operations of the JDC, I mentioned this difference and Mo, as we all knew him, said, "Don't you see why? When you went to see him in Rhodes, Bunche was the No. 2 man, the aide to Bernadotte, and it was his responsibility to remind Bernadotte about the terms of the agreement, all the rules and regulations that he had to remember and be aware of should he decide to act otherwise. It was Bunche's role to keep him apprised. However, once Bunche became the No. 1 man, he could do as he saw fit, knowing the regulations but also knowing that eventual policy rested with him. That's why the Bunche you knew in Rhodes was different from the Bunche the Arabs and Israelis knew later who received the Nobel Prize." Mo's words always remained with me, for within my own position in the JDC and later on in other organizations, there were times when I was an aide and times when I was the chief. I kept the distinction between the two roles very clear.

Bernadotte's assassin was never found. To this day, no one knows

71

who did it, although many conjectures filled the air for months and years. My experience with this man was highly positive, one which bespoke a genuine humanitarianism and obvious sympathy for the searchers of peace, and I think in his mind I was included among the latter. He and Bunche both played their roles; they both have honorable places in modern Jewish history.

Passover Seders

Soon after the camps had been opened, the Palestinian Committee for the Cyprus Exiles was organized under the leadership of Moshe Brachman. Its purpose was to help the internees in whatever manner it could, modest though it might be.

Brachman often came to Cyprus to find out what his committee could do. It sent extra food; it sent some cultural materials, Passover Haggadahs, for instance, and, was also extremely useful in keeping Palestinians involved in the fates of those in Cyprus.

Passover 1947 was an event to remember because Brachman came up with something special. He wanted to send fresh carp. He planned to have a boat loaded with properly iced carp, grown in various carp pools and miniature lakes in Palestinian kibbutzim, and to dispatch it from Haifa on Thursday in time for arrival early on Friday morning, the eve of Pesakh (Passover). I thought it was a great idea.

I went to the British authorities to enlist their cooperation. Among other things, I wanted people to stand by and wait for the boat so that the carp could be brought to the camp as quickly as possible. *Erev* Pesakh fell on Friday, and one could not cook after sundown since it was also the Sabbath.

internees, about 10,000 of them, and the British readily agreed to string electric lights so that the Seder could be properly illuminated. (We had no electricity in the camps and the evenings were lighted by lanterns, lux lamps, and other devices.) The British readily cooperated and I was very grateful to them. Brachman came up with another idea to which we quickly agreed and did everything possible to realize. He suggested that personalities from the Jewish Community of Palestine come to Cyprus for the Seder to show the solidarity between them and the internees. Leading personalities did come, among them Itzchak Ben-Zvi (at that time head of the Jewish Community of Palestine), the Chief Rabbi of Haifa, and other important guests. *Erev* Pesakh came. The lorries were ready, waiting at the Famagusta harbor for the boat to arrive from Haifa at 8 A.M. It did not come at 8, nor at 9, nor at 10. It had been held up by mechanical defects and could not arrive until 2 PM.

I was jumping out of my skin because, as I've said, if the carp arrived at the camp too late, it could not be cooked and all the wonderful planning would have been in vain. The British, too, were impatient. It was Good Friday and their soldiers were spending the day at the Famagusta harbor in idle waiting.

Once the boat arrived, the lorries were loaded quickly and sped to the camp in the nick of time. Nobody was forced to violate the Sabbath.

I recall an elderly man talking to me and weeping over the carp. "Do you know," he said to me, "this is the first time since before the war that I actually see a carp—fresh carp, like the ones which used to adorn our Friday night and holiday tables throughout my life."

The carp was a minor element in the celebration of the Seder out in the open for 10,000 persons. The Hagaddah was read. Obviously, the 10,000 persons had to be scattered all over the camp and we moved from place to place.

The Chief Rabbi of Haifa was greeted as a Chief Rabbi should be, as were all the other dignitaries. All of us felt good.

We took special pride in having been able to pull it off, to have a real Seder, graced by luminaries who came to express their support to their less fortunate fellows.

Among the personalities who attended the event was I.F. Stone. He had come from Haifa to Famagusta as a reporter on one of the British naval vessels and was admitted to the camp. He introduced himself to me. Of course I had heard of him. He was a writer for *PM*, a New York newspaper, and I offered a guide to accompany him around the camp. Stone turned to me gruffly, "Don't give me any Jewish Agency tours. I'll take care of myself."

I thought to myself, "Brother, if that's the way you want it, that's the way you'll have it," and left him alone. He disappeared for a day or two, and when he came to see me it was after he had spent time wandering around the camp. He had gone from tent to tent interviewing people. He had slept overnight with one of the families. He did a thorough job of investigating how the camp was run, who the people were, what the JDC did, what the people thought of the JDC and of the camp committee, and what their hopes were. He wrote up his findings in a six-day serial which appeared for a whole week in *PM*, accompanied by photographs taken by Alex Taylor who escorted Stone on this trip.

Stone's story was highly complimentary to the JDC, and the gruffness which he had displayed disappeared as soon as he had finished his investigations. We became friends.

A further word about Ben-Zvi. Tall, dignified, and slender, he became later the second President of Israel. At that time, Passover 1947, he was the head of the Jewish Community (*Vaad Leumi*), the defacto government of the Jews in Palestine.

I arranged for him to have a room at the Savoy Hotel in Famagusta, where I also stayed. It was 2 A.M., after the Seder, when we left the camp. Caraolos was three miles from Famagusta and I had my chauffeur waiting to take Ben-Zvi to the hotel. Ben-Zvi politely declined. "I am the head of the Jewish Cummunity," he said. "I do not ride on the Sabbath." So he and I walked slowly to the Savoy Hotel. We talked about Cyprus, about Palestine, about him, about me, about many things. He stands out as a giant. In addition to his many virtues, his modesty was remarkable; he was one of the most modest men I have ever met.

The Seder of Passover 1947 was an unforgettable Seder. I remember it and I know that many Israelis and fellow Cyprus internees remember it. I have met them through the years and they have told me so. It was a great day. I was grateful to the British for their cooperation and sent them several cases of wine. They loved Adom Atik, a Palestine wine, and thanked me for this gesture.

We had one more Passover in camp, the Passover of 1948. Again, an outdoor Seder was arranged, and again we had visitors from Palestine, among them Shoshana Damari, a very popular singer whose family had originally come from Yemen. She went from table to table singing many melodies, including some Yiddish ones which she had learned especially for this occasion.

Singer Shoshana Damari performing at Caraolos camp.

I asked Damari whether she would visit the Jewish wing of the
British Military Hospital in Nicosia and she readily consented. During the week we went to the BMH, where the patients occupied six
wards, and, to save her energies, I wanted to assemble the patients
who could be moved in a common courtyard to hear her. Damari
insisted on going to each of the wards and singing in all six of them.
Her listeners, all in bed, applauded with gratitude, gasping in
astonishment at Damari, the Yemenite, who sang Yiddish songs. For
them, as for us, Damari symbolized the integration of cultures
toward which Palestine was striving. It was the first time I had ever
met her. When she later made concert tours in the United States we
met again, and often recalled the thrill of her performance on Passover
at the BMH in Nicosia.

By I. F. Stone Passover in Cyprus' Nissen Huts

*I. F. Stone, PM correspondent, was turned back by Cyprus quarantine offi-
cials recently when he arrived on a ship deporting "illegal" Jewish immigrants
from Palestine, despite the fact that he had a British visa for Cyprus. Now Stone
has got into the Cyprus internment camps—his dispatch does not reveal how,
although it apparently was by air.*

EN ROUTE FROM CYPRUS TO PALESTINE, Apr. 7.—This is being
written 3000 feet up over the blue Mediterranean in a tiny four-passen-
ger two-motored mosquito-like plane bound for Haifa from Nicosia in
Cyprus where I have just spent the first two days of the Passover in
camps established by the British to intern "illegal" Jewish immigrants seized in
Palestine.

There are two sets of camps on the sweet-smelling ancient Greek Isle of
Cyprus for 11,300 refugees now held there, one at Caraolos and the other at
Xylotybou, and both are being enlarged to meet the expected Spring rush of
Aliyah Beth (illegal immigration) boats which will probably boost the Jewish
population to 20,000 before the end of June.

I took the first *seder* (passover ceremonial dinner) Friday night in the middle section of a Nissen hut, housing three families in its three single-room dwell-
ings. My host was Moshe Efrati, a 35-year-old Romanian Jew who had arrived
in Palestine on the *Keneseth Israel* in February with his wife, Rachel, daughter
Miriam, 15, and son Eliezer, 12.

Efrati, a *yeshivah bachur* (seminary student) until 22, was a laundryman by
trade, a religious Jew and a member of the Agudath Israel.

Unexpected Guests
Are Made Welcome

When Alex Taylor, American Jewish Joint Distribution Committee camera-
man and an old friend of mine, dropped in on the Efrati family, the *seder* had
already begun. We came unexpected and unannounced, but were at once made
welcome. The room with its curved, corrugated tin roof, was lit by a lantern
on the table and two small candles stuck in a tin can full of sand in the middle
of the traditional *seder* repast—wine, matzoths, bitter herbs, hard-boiled eggs
and salt-water sauce for them.

Father Efrati sat at the head of the table, reclining on a pillow as is customary for the *seder*, his hat set on the back of his head, without a tie, but in
a clean shirt and wearing a jacket. He was lean-faced and brown.

On his right, sat his bright-eyed son of 12, wearing a tiny *yarmelka* (skull
cap), and already a student in the *yeshivah* (theological seminary) organized
by religious Jews in the camp. On the father's left sat his good wife and daughter.
Alex and I were given *haggadas* (Passover service books) and the *seder* went
on. It was no hop-skip-and-jump affair, as is customary in most American Jewish
homes. Efrati left nothing out. We rose to drink our wine with blessings, partook
of the bitter herbs and first matzohs. Efrati sang the parts with relish and explained and translated as he went along, in Yiddish for the benefit of the visitors
and his wife and daughter.

The mother looked on as if she didn't know how one man could be so bright
and the daughter was fascinated while the son's eyes shone. For them it was
a fairy tale and religious service and personal story, this story of the exodus from
Egypt. For them the ancient cruel taskmasters were no fable: they had been

in slave labor camps under German occupation. For them, the God who smote the Egyptians was the same God who brought the Third Reich low. And were they not like the Jews under Moses? Moses went through one kind of wilderness or another to the promised land? And as Efrati explained in his own running commentary to the service, comfortingly, "We had to go down into Egypt for 400 years, but we need only be six months or so in Cyprus."

Unfortunately, as more "illegal" immigrants pile up behind the double barbed wire fences and heavily timbered gates of the Cyprus camps, it will take 18 months before the latest arrivals get their chance to go to Palestine under the present British quota of 1500 a month, half for Cyprus, half for the British zone DPs in Germany and Austria.

In the meantime 11,000 human beings, including 1400 children, must go on living in two vast settlements of Nissen huts,-the ugliest architecture known to mankind—a sort of tin igloo with cement flooring set in bleak rows on the level grassless plots near the sea, each settlement divided into several encampments with a fringe of tents, surrounded with barbed wire and a row of latrines whose smell, when the wind is in the right direction, easily overcomes the orange blossoms which pervade Cyprus at this season. It is not exactly a Summer resort, but the people in it are not pathetic, miserable wretches.

Babies Are Born,
Couples Are Married

Life flows on strong, and vigorous babies are being born at the rate of 30 to 40 monthly. There have been almost 600 weddings since the camps were established last August and there were 135 nuptials during the two weeks before Passover.

There are schools and synagogues, camp newspapers, an art exhibition, workshops and several soccer teams which often play the British guards and boast they have never been beaten. Forty per cent of the Jews in the camp are Hungarians and Romanians, most of the remainder Polish, but with a scattering of others from England to Morocco—which is represented by four native Jews—and Egypt, which supplied one. I tell no secret when I say that occasionally one encounters some young American who volunteered to help escort the less fortunate to Palestine. So most of the population are young and husky.

I arrived, of course, at an unusually happy time. The Passover has a deep personal meaning for these Jews. In co-operation, the Yishuv (Jewish community of Palestine) and the American Joint Distribution Committee, which practically runs these camps under British supervision, brought in 45 tons of matzoths, 10,000 bottles of wines; 40,000 eggs, three tons of fish, almost three tons of sausage, plus candles, prayer books and special ritual vegetables like horseradish for seders. And there was a delegation of visiting actors and political celebrities from Palestine including Ben Zvi, President of Vaad Leumi, the Jewish National Council, to cheer the internees.

In darkness as the soldiers examined our passes and lifted the heavy timber gates for us to enter, all looked dimly lit and desolate. But this first impression soon gave way to a festive feeling as we came upon one seder celebration after another; some in family groups like Efrati's, some huge kibbutzim (collectives), making merry in one big Nissen hut.

And there were enormous open air seders, notably that of Youth Aliyah where I found Mrs. de Sola Pool, American Hadassah executive, surrounded by happy children, Jewish orphans gathered together from all over Europe by Hadassah for immigration to Palestine. Mrs. de Sola Pool had just discovered the camp cooks were using artichokes as flowers, and had taught them how to cook the unfamiliar vegetable. The camps resounded with singing and there were horas (communal dances) everywhere until late at night.

Distinguished Visitors

Besides the weekend lecturers and the guests on Passover, we had special visitors from time to time, a man or a woman of great distinction, who felt it necessary to see the situation on Cyprus personally and to assure the people in the camp that everything was being done to hasten their release. I would like to speak about six such persons from among the many: Chief Rabbi Uziel of Palestine, Rabbi Semiatitzky of London, Golda Meir (then Meyerson), Sidov Belarsky, Mrs. Tamar DeSola Pool, and Dr. Joseph J. Schwartz.

Rabbi Uziel and Rabbi Semiatitzky

Rabbi Meir Uziel was the Sephardic chief rabbi of Palestine and he and Rabbi Herzog, the Ashkenazic chief rabbi, occupied their respective offices during the Cyprus period. The institution of the office of chief rabbi was brought into being by the mandate government which recognized the existence in Palestine of two separate communities, the Ashkenazi and the Sephardi, each with its own traditions and customs. Two men were appointed to serve them: the Ashkenazic chief rabbi was known as such, while the Sephardic chief rabbi was called the "first in Zion."

Chief Rabbi Uziel notified me that he was coming to visit Cyprus. He did not need my help in getting permission, he was able to do it directly through the mandate government. I met him at the airport and took him directly to my house to talk about Cyprus, to ask him what he wanted to do, and to offer my services. Rabbi Uziel was an impressive man, somewhat above middle height, dark eyes, with a neatly trimmed gray beard and an aura of dignity about him.

As I served tea, it was interesting to note that neither he nor Rabbi Semiatitzky, of whom I shall tell later, brought up the question of *Kashruth*. However, I was aware of their feelings and made sure to use a glass tea set and to serve frumine crackers made by the famous biscuit firm in Palestine. I told Rabbi Uziel that we had only about 1,000 Sephardim among the 30-odd-thousand persons in camp at the time. Rabbi Uziel indicated that while he was naturally interested in them, his concern was not purely parochial and that he would like to see and speak to everybody, if possible. I had announced his visit and nearly all the people in the camp were excited and waited impatiently.

His presence was magnetic. He wore the customary rabbinic turban of the Sephardim and a long silk caftan. His language was primarily Hebrew, but now and then he spoke French or English. Everywhere he was received with open arms, and everywhere he praised the internees for their courage and determination to come to Palestine, assuring them that the Jews of Palestine, as well as the Jews of the world, were doing everything they could to hasten their release. The *Neturei Karta* (an ultra-Orthodox sect) did not receive him well. In fact, they scoffed at him, jeered at him, and some even spat in his path. I was humiliated, blushed for shame and began to mumble words of apology, but Rabbi Uziel quietly assured me that this was nothing new to him; the *Neturei Karta* acted this way in Palestine all the time, yet they, too, are Jews and they, too, must be helped without regard for their actions against him. Once again, the lesson that all Jews are united in fellowship took on special meaning, particularly on this occasion.

Rabbi Uziel's visit meant a great deal. It showed the internees that everybody, including the highest religious authorities, was deeply concerned and tried to hasten the day of their departure from Cyprus.

Rabbi Meir Uziel speaks to a group of internees.

I received a cable one day from Rabbi Semiatitzky of London, a member of the rabbinic court in that city, stating that he was coming to Cyprus and that he had received permission to bring 500 Yeshiva students to Palestine outside the quota. This permission had been granted to him by the British authorities in London.

After his arrival I brought him first to my house, and, over cups of tea, we talked. Rabbi Semiatitzky was the very model of a rabbi who was not a Hassid. His skulcap was not the kind of cap one sees today, but the cubical black yarmulke worn especially by Lithuanian Jews. He was a man of great charm and wit and impressed one by his appearance, twinkling eyes and longish greying beard. He wore a kind of tuxedo coat typical of the rabbinic garb I was familiar with from America, where it was used by orthodox rabbis who had come from abroad.

Rabbi Semiatitzky told me that the British had acceded to his request for the special grant of 500 extra-quota emigres out of Cyprus and he was here to carry this out. "After all," he said, "the ransom of captives" is a command. Unfortunately, throughout Jewish history captives were taken by marauding nations and it was incumbent upon other Jews to free them for ransom. In addition, a student of the Torah takes priority over others in the matter of ransoming of captives. I explained to Rabbi Semiatitzky that, while he may have easily convinced the British authorities in London, his task in Cyprus would not be as easy, for here he would have to deal with the Central Committee, which has as its guideline, "first in, first out." The only exceptions ever made were those on the request of the emissaries for persons specially needed by the *Hagannah* or upon the request of the *Mossad* for the release of sailors and others who, in the opinion of the *Mossad*, had to leave immediately. "Besides," I said, "not everybody on the Central committee would understand your *halakhic* imperatives." Many of them had never studied or had studied very little. They were ignoramuses in Jewish law. There were a few learned Jews, but they were scoffers and unbelievers and had long ago discarded their faith even though they still retained great knowledge of the Torah. Rabbi Semiatitzky, with a twinkle in his eye, said to me that he must try nevertheless; he was sure he would prevail, especially with the scoffers, for traditionally, he reminded me, it is better to be an *apikoros* (unbeliever) than an *am ha'aretz* (an ignoramus). By the same token, it would be easier to talk to an *apikoros* than to an *am ha'aretz*.

I brought the rabbi to camp and, after an initial tour, he spent his time with the Committee in pursuit of his purpose. He also met many other Jews, but his primary purpose was to select Yeshiva men, and in fact he spent two weeks with the Central Committee talking, arguing, negotiating, until finally an agreement was reached. Each side compromised and 500 people did leave on this extra-quota—250 Yeshiva men and 250 selected by the Central Committee. His visit, I am sure, made as deep an impression on the people in the camp, even on his so-called antagonists, as it did on me. One could not but be moved by his wisdom, integrity, wit, and by his love of the Jews.

Golda Meyerson

In November 1947, Golda Meyerson came to camp. She notified us in advance. She, too, did not need our intervention; she received her permission directly from the Palestine authorities. The fact that Golda Meyerson was coming sent an electric wave throughout the camp. Everyone knew who she was and everyone was aware of her decades of work as a leader in Zionism, Palestine, the *Histadrut*, the Labor Party and the Jewish Agency. She was at the time, and for years later until her death, a foremost woman in Palestine, later in Israel, taking her place in the very top group of Jewish leaders. As was usual with other visitors, Mrs. Meyerson, or Golda as we all called her, began her visit at my home. She came to breakfast and my wife, Eve, served a typical American breakfast: fresh orange juice, cold cereal and milk, eggs, toast and marmalade and coffee. Golda seemed to be particularly taken with the cereal and the coffee, and with us as a family. She was relaxed and very quickly dispelled any sense of distance caused by the natural deference we felt towards her. She admired my wife for her work as hostess to one and all, as our house was always open not only to visitors but, more importantly, to members of the staff. There was rarely a meal, even breakfast, without one or two guests and sometimes more, for social and business reasons. She was intrigued by the fact that my two sons—Levi, then going on nine, and Marc, a little over four—were both studying at the camp and thought that this was wonderful. I

Golda Meyerson visiting Camp 55 in Caraolos, November 1947.

personally saw nothing wonderful about it. Where else could they
study? The schools in Famagusta were Greek and obviously out of
the question for them. The only other school was a private English
school and I certainly would not send the boys there, so they went to
the camp—besides, if it was good enough for thousands of other
children, it ought to be good enough for them. Levi quickly learned
Hebrew. Marc mingled with children of many nationalities in the
nursery school and kindergarten that he attended; he played with
them and made friends with them, even though there was a Babel of
languages.

We worked out a plan for Golda's appearance in camp and we tried
to follow it. First of all, it involved her speaking to as many persons in
the camp as possible. She did so, speaking three or four times in
various places before thousands of people. She spoke in Yiddish,
expressed her solidarity, explained the issue for them, and urged the
persons in camp to make one more sacrifice. There was a danger of an
epidemic of typhus among the children, especially among the infants, and Golda asked persons without infants voluntarily to give up
their rightful turn and allow the infants and their families to leave.
Some demurred, but only a few; everybody else understood the

need to do so and the fact that it was Golda who asked for it was enough to convince them that it should be done.

A reception was organized indoors for Golda, for the staff and the emissaries. She and I were the only two speakers. I introduced her; I spoke in Hebrew, perhaps the second or third time in my life, welcomed her and indicated that "the boundaries between the JDC and the Jewish Agency have been blurred and our aims are now merged." I remember these words particularly because Golda used them as the basic topic for her remarks. She said there was a time when the JDC and the Jewish Agency were at odds. The Jewish Agency through the United Palestine Appeal in America pressed for aid to Palestine solely or primarily, and the JDC insisted that Jews everywhere ought to be helped—in Palestine too, of course, but Jews of Europe and other places must not be overlooked. In fact, the JDC began its work when first organized in 1914 in Palestine, but later it became the major relief organization for Jews throughout the world, and its stress on work for Jews outside of Palestine continued through the second World War period and until *Aliya Bet* began. The strength of Dr. Schwartz's conviction and the force of his personality—Dr. J. Schwartz was the Director General of the JDC for Overseas Operations—led to an ever closer cooperation with the Jewish Agency and even towards the financing of some of its so-called illegal activities. On Cyprus there was almost perfect harmony between the two organizations, so much so that while we kept our financial books apart, the workers were true comrades in arms, the aims were the same, the goal was a unified one: get the Jews out of Cyprus as quickly as possible. Golda elaborated on this subject and encouraged us to carry on. Her visit was unforgettable to all of us and to Golda too, for many years later at the celebration of the 20th anniversary of Malben, the special JDC agency in Israel, Golda spoke about the JDC work on Cyprus, about me and about Josh Leibner. In camp Golda Meyerson represented the very meaning of her name—a golden heart, a person who shed light, who was radiant.

Sidor Belarsky

Sidor Belarsky also visited Cyprus. A famous singer of Yiddish folk songs, Belarsky also sang cantorial music and Hebrew melodies. He was in great demand and was loved by all.

Soon after Chief Rabbi Uziel, Belarsky came at his own request. I was delighted, of course, to have him and got him the necessary permission. He arrived on a Friday and we determined that the following evening, soon after the end of the Sabbath, he would give a concert in Caraolos. We had no stage or concert hall and Belarsky suggested that he sing from the platform of a truck. All he needed was a piano and a pianist. The Savoy Hotel in Famagusta had a little string orchestra and a pianist whom we hired as Belarsky's accompanist. We brought the piano from the hotel, but, much to our dismay, the piano was out of tune and the pianist was out of touch, sadly lacking the qualities that make a good accompanist. There was nothing we could do; Belarsky berated himself for not bringing his own accompanist but the concert proceeded. Thousands of people came to hear him. There was a deep hush. He sang without a mike, and his voice was resonant enough to carry to the very last rows. He sang chiefly in Yiddish, classic Yiddish songs such as "Rozhenkes mit Mandlen"; ghetto and partisan songs such as "Zug Nit Kein Mol Az du Geyst Dem Letzten Veg" ("Never say that you are treading your last path") by Mordecai Gebeirtig, the great Polish song writer and composer; Hebrew melodies such as "Kinneret," made famous by Belarsky himself; cantorial music and some Russian songs. The crowd would not let him go, demanding encore after encore, which Belarsky gave. People could be seen with tears streaming down their faces and in introducing the songs Belarsky himself was choked with emotion. His songs took on greater meaning and pathos than usual. I have heard Belarsky since then many times and listen avidly to his records; that night in Caraolos was unmatched. Years later Belarsky told me this and whenever we met he spoke of the night he sang from the platform of a truck to the people behind barbed wire.

Tamar DeSola Pool

Mrs. Tamar DeSola Pool of New York was a leader in the Hadassah movement. During the Cyprus period, her work was concerned with the Hadassah Hospital and the Medical School and with raising money for both organizations. She was the wife of Rabbi David DeSola Pool, the leading Sephardic rabbi of the United States and the occupant of the pulpit of the Spanish and Portugese Synagogue in New York City, the oldest Jewish congregation in the new world. Dr. DeSola Pool had an international reputation as a scholar and communal leader and Mrs. DeSola Pool's fame also grew from year to year as the great Hadassah leader.

She wanted to come to Cyprus to see personally what the situation of the young was in the camps. I quickly arranged her trip, and while she came to stay for a day or so, she stayed a whole week. In walking through the Caraolos camps she noticed that the tents were not particularly clean and the meals were not well prepared; she felt she could do something about it. Originally communal kitchens had been set up, but they were very soon disbanded because the internees preferred to prepare their own meals. They used gas stoves provided by the JDC, while the food was issued by the British and supplemented by the JDC. Mrs. Pool felt that she could help the women and men by showing them how to keep a tent clean and how to cook, and literally rolled her sleeves up and went from tent to tent to spend an hour or so in each, teaching them how to cook, showing them new recipes and helping them clean up the camp. She did that for an entire week. Those of us who observed the great Hadassah leader doing all these chores were overwhelmed with wonder. Her presence and what she did strengthened us.

Dr. Schwartz

Dr. Joseph J. Schwartz was the Director General for Overseas Operations for the JDC during the Cyprus period. I had known him since the spring of 1945, when I asked him to come to Athens to see what measures the JDC could take to alleviate the immediate needs of 10,000 Jewish survivors out of the original 100,000 that lived in Greece before the Nazi invasion. His trip to Athens brought about a friendship which lasted till the end of his days.

As long ago as 1946, Dr. Schwartz was a legendary figure and in the following years his accomplishments were to grow fabulously. A rabbi and son of a rabbi, he took his doctorate in Semitics at Yale, served for a short while in a pulpit, taught German at Long Island University, and studied in Cairo. He then became Director of the Brooklyn Federation of Jewish Charities and, when that organization merged with the one in Manhattan to become the Federation of Jewish Philanthropies in New York, he was appointed Associate Director. From that position he went on to the JDC. He was sent abroad in '38 or '39 to assist Morris Troper, then the Director General of the JDC, and when Troper was called to Washington to help in the American war effort, Schwartz became the Director General. Tall, spare, soft-spoken and quiet, he was always on the move. He met with Jewish leaders and Jews in general wherever possible to find out how the JDC could help them. His very presence, his sharp angular face, his deep eyes and jutting lips bespoke authority, an authority ingrained and natural to him. Those of us who worked with him learned to love him. His zeal was contagious, his example had to be followed. I shall never forget the days in the summer and fall of 1945, while I was stationed in Paris awaiting assignment to a post in Italy, when I felt filled with the passion and pride of being a part of the JDC team. It was at night that those of us who were in Paris would meet in Dr. Schwartz's hotel room, have a drink and talk. The conversation, though occasionally personal, dealt mainly with the problems facing the Jews of Europe whom we had come to help. Telephone calls would come in constantly from all parts of Europe asking for Schwartz, so that he could hear the latest troubles and the proposals for help. He would discuss these calls immediately with us and, as we all talked, we had the feeling that we were not only observers, but active participants in the making of Jewish history.

I saw Dr. Schwartz in Paris at Country Directors' conferences twice before he came to the island, accompanied by his secretary, Melvin Goldstein. For the Leibners and me, it was a great day. He came to both our homes. I even induced him to borrow a pair of shorts and take a swim. It was good to see Dr. Schwartz relax. I recall

86

the amusing incident involving the meals that Eve and Pnina Leibner served in our respective homes. He visited us first, and we served chicken thinking it would be a good change after the austerity food program in Palestine whence he had come. As it turned out, he had had chicken and nothing but chicken in Jerusalem. Eve quickly told Pnina, who changed her whole menu and hurried to get steaks instead of the chicken she too had prepared.

Schwartz did not come to see us; he had come to see the camps. He walked through them slowly, taking in everything, and was amazed at what he saw. Nothing in his work had prepared him for the sight of the thousands of persons who were not really in a concentration camp nor really in a displaced persons' camp, but nevertheless in a camp which was behind barbed wire, administered differently from other camps, yet guarded by the British who were presumably antagonists, a camp helped by the JDC, but actually run by the internees. Many knew Dr. Schwartz. They had seen him in displaced persons' camps and thousands had seen him in Constanza, Rumania, when the Pan ships were being loaded with some 15,000 passengers. He recognized that if the JDC was to be true to its slogan of relief, rescue and rehabilitation, then the desires of the thousands of Jews of Europe who felt that those three R's could best be achieved in Palestine had to be met. It was the JDC's task to help meet these desires even if it meant working with organizations that were not particularly concerned with legalities and the usual restraints. His aim was to bring Jews to Palestine regardless of what any other nation, primarily the British, might think or do.

That was why Schwartz had been at Constanza and Jews in camp recognized him. Upon seeing him, they began pouring out their troubles. Why were they in camp so long? Couldn't something be done to get them out? Demands were made—more clothes, more food, shoes, housing. The opportunity of his presence was not missed and complaints were made even against the staff. He listened, tried to calm people, and later when he met with Leibner and me alone he asked whether we couldn't meet some of the demands. I indicated that if we tried to meet them on our own, that would relieve the British of the responsibilities which in reality lay primarily with them. While Dr. Schwartz agreed, he nevertheless advised me to spend a little more money, which he supplied. I made some remarks about some of the grumblers: they were known in camp as the "rich" ones. They had managed to smuggle money out of Rumania and had diamonds imbedded in their teeth, which could be found only by very careful inspection. Dr. Schwartz's response was that, rich or not, they were prisoners; if we could meet their grievances, by all means let's do so. It revealed one of his great qualities: compassion for all and an impulse to convert compassion into action.

A personal note. During his three-day visit, Dr. Schwartz said to me, "I hear that your house is a gathering place for staff and that Eve and you have made it an open house for everyone at all times of the day." "True," I said. Apart from the formalities of the Savoy Hotel, there was no other place for the staff to relax except for the staff room in the camp. I didn't blame staff members for wanting to come out of the camp; they worked there, ate there, slept there; it was good to get away once in a while. Schwartz listened and when he left he said, "Don't forget to send us a bill for your entertainment expenses." I demurred, not because we couldn't use the money, but because I felt this was an intrusion, the commercialization of a friendly act. Schwartz insisted, and henceforth the JDC office in Paris paid for the entertainment in our home. This in no way reduced our feeling of comradeship, but it indicated, once again, how sensitive Schwartz was even to such needs, and how grateful he was when they were met by his staff.

Later Dr. Schwartz took on the directorship of the United Jewish Appeal and then of Israel Bonds, but his interest in the Joint Distribution Committee remained strong for the rest of his life. He served as its vice-chairman and as one of its officers, and was active in its work until his death. In Joseph Schwartz the JDC had a truly great leader, great in his own right, the right man at the right place at the right time.

The Rites of Passage

Births, Marriages, Deaths

Over 50,000 people went through the camps on Cyprus over a period of more than two years. The important events in life, those which sociologists call "the rites of passage", births, marriages, and deaths, were accompanied by the ritual ceremonies. However, on Cyprus, they took on a special poignancy; everything went on behind barbed wire or under guard.

Births. I don't know the exact figures, but at least 2,000 people can claim the Cyprus camps as their birthplace. Generally, a woman was delivered of her child in the Jewish wing of the British Military Hospital in Nicosia, though sometimes a birth took place within the camp. Every birth was a reason to celebrate; life cannot be stopped.

At least 1,000 males were born and all of them underwent the rite of circumcision. I regarded it as a very great honor to be asked to be the *sandak* at a birth. It is the *sandak* who holds the child while the act of circumcision is performed by the *mohel,* or the circumciser. Usually, this honor is given to an elderly person, the grandfather of the child or some other distinguished graybeard. At one of these ceremonies, I found myself, at the age of 38, sitting in a *kittle* (white caftan) and being a *sandak.* A few years ago, when I saw the *mohel* of the camps, who now lives in Allentown, Pennsylvania, he showed me pictures of acts of circumcision, including of one in which I acted as a *sandak.*

Marriages. Even behind barbed wire many marriages took place. Most marriages were between internees or between a staff member and an internee; others were between staff members.

The first two kinds had to be celebrated inside the camp, and the traditional *hupah* (canopy) was held over bride and groom outdoors.

89

"Under the Wedding Canopy."

A cup of wine was drunk and the ritual glass shattered in recognition, even in times of joy, that we must always remember Jerusalem; and then the *mazal tovs* and the celebrations would go on and on late into the night.

In Cyprus the shattering of the glass took on a poignant meaning. Here, Jerusalem was remembered on its very threshold and the usual hope that Jerusalem would one day rise up in glory again was redoubled.

One of the boats coming into port, the *Chaim Arlosoroff*, had a unique group of immigrants, 800 young women from Sweden, where they had been living either during or immediately after the war and were now on their way to Palestine. Think of it. A sudden infusion of 800 young women. Love affairs blossomed overnight and marriage after marriage took place. And here, too, JDC men fell in love with the newcomers and were married right in camp.

Elie Moyal, the emissary to the Sephardim, married my secretary, Shoshana Yoshpe. Dr. Rappaport married Lilka in a wedding that took place in my home. Emmanuel Gutmann, then a teacher, married Nahamah Foreman, then a nurse. I have kept in touch with all these people and with many more. The late Dr. Rappaport was one of the leading cardiologists in Israel. Moyal is a political leader, Gutmann is a professor of Social Administration at the Hebrew University and Nahamah Foreman, his wife, the chief of nursing for Northern Israel. I am sure that others, as the years have gone by, have grown in position, stature, and prominence. Yet, when I meet any of them, or when we have a reunion in Israel, as is the custom, we get to talking about Cyprus and, in spite of the difficulties of the time, those days still appear as the highlight of their careers.

Deaths. Life includes death. The death of 400 people occurred on Cyprus . Most of them were aged. An infant was occasionally stillborn and sometimes a younger person died of a grave illness. Burial was in the Jewish cemetery in Cyprus, known as Margoa, which in Hebrew means "rest".

After the camps closed, some of us went to pay our last respects to those for whom Cyprus became the eternal resting place. We laid wreaths upon the tombstones, said *kaddish,* and bade a final farewell.

While there I noticed something which shook me. The tombstones made in camp had many an error—not statistical errors, for

91

I'm sure the dates of birth and death were correct—but in spelling and other evidences indicating that they were the work of persons not literate. I informed our office in Palestine and eventually a committee was sent from Palestine to Cyprus to inspect the tomb-stones and to correct all the errors. I could not rest until the corrections were made, for though the dead were at peace, I could not make peace with myself and allow this blemish on the last evidence of Jewish internment on Cyprus. I have never been to Cyprus since the camps closed. I hope to go one day, and I shall go to Margoa once again, and say *kaddish* for those who are eternally at peace.

A Jewish Agency Representative and Morris Laub, before leaving in February, 1949, lay wreaths on graves of internees buried on Cyprus.

Celebrations

In addition to observing the holidays and celebrating a *simka* (a birth or a wedding), there was a monthly celebration marking the departure of the 750 persons whose turn had come to leave. The goodbyes were touching. Everyone was happy to see the fortunate ones go, though friendships had to be interrupted (hopefully temporarily).

The scene was a frantic one: persons busily packing, others making the rounds to say farewell, a last handshake with us and those of us who had special relationships, and a fervent wish on the part of those who were leaving that soon the long hoped-for-day would arrive and the others would leave too.

A special touch to these celebrations I wish to mention. How it began I do not know, but as long as the person who was involved was in camp, it continued. He was a violinist, and as people lined up to leave the camp, he stood and played his violin—sad songs and happy, a medley of melodies, and occasionally a classical piece. This was his way of saying goodbye. It was a symbol that those who came to the island in tears, in anger, and in fury, were now leaving accompanied by cheer, joyous farewells, and music.

Three other occasions called for massive celebrations, one of them on November 29, 1947, the day on which the United Nations resolution on the partition of Palestine was adopted. The Jewish world was in favor of partition, although it would mean a much smaller area for the Jewish state; the leaders in Palestine and at the United Nations were ready to accept a much smaller territory if this would bring the possibility of living in peace with their neighbors. As we know now, nothing came of this resolution: the partition was rejected by the Arabs, and the fight for the Jewish state went on.

But on November 29, 1947, the vote in the UN had real meaning, it implied the recognition of the Jewish state, and hopefully with it the closing of the camps.

93

A fiddler sends off the internees with a tune as they depart for Palestine.

A holiday celebration. The sign reads "Blessed are you in the city, blessed are you in the field."

News got around very quickly in the camp. Even though radios were forbidden by the British, almost everyone had a litle portable radio, sometimes even a bigger one. The radios were bought by Rivka Kehana and smuggled into camp or else given to various people by the emissaries or even by the *Haganah*.

Radio was the means of communication with the world and the most reliable way of knowing what was going on. As this had been true for the ghetto fighters during the war, who in the secrecy of their bunkers used to listen to the BBC every day and find out the truth (different from what the Nazi guards and torturers had been telling them), so it was now for the internees on Cyprus. The news of the UN vote on November 29th spread like wildfire. In fact, the internees had cabled their demand for partition, which was read aloud there. Obviously, when the vote came, we knew the outcome immediately.

I was at home at the time, but made my way quickly to the camp. I was sure there would be a celebration and I wanted to be a part of it.

November is usually rainy on Cyprus. What had been dry, hard paths were turned by the rain into mud, but nothing could stop the hora dancing, the singing, the cheers, and the joy; nothing could flag the energy of the internees. They danced all night.

The next day there was an open meeting. I spoke to the internees in Yiddish and pointed out to them how certain months of the year take on special meaning through historical events. Hannukah was celebrated that year during the month of November, and the UN made the 29th a date to remember ever after together with November 2, Balfour Day.

Independence Day, May 15, 1948, was the day of the declaration of independence by the State of Israel. On Cyprus the radios brought the news and the celebrations began. If people danced with joy on November 29th, 1947, how is one to describe the frenzied joy of that night in camp? In referring to the water-drawing festival, which took place when the temple was still standing, the Talmud says that "He who has never seen the festival of libation has never really seen a celebration." He who has never seen the celebration on Cyprus of the declaration of Israel's independence has never known what it is possible for a celebration to be. By May 15th, the slushy roads and paths had hardened again and everybody was out dancing, with ever renewed frenzy, all night once again. I remember one of

95

the emissaries who had become a friend of mine: a quiet soft-spoken man in his 50's with whom I never associated joy or merriment. That night he was a different man. He danced and danced and danced and sang and sang and sang incessantly. Watching him, one couldn't help but become infected with his excitement. Watching him, I became worried, for hour after hour of dancing and hopping and cheering and singing at the top of his voice would surely have its effects. I asked him to take a rest and he pulled me into the circle yelling, "Rest? Today? Tonight? This is the greatest day of my life! Come on, join us!" And I did, but young as I was, younger than he, and filled with merriment, I had to rest after a half-hour or so. Covered with sweat, I had to sit down and cool off.

The merriment in camp was accompanied by the hope of immediate release. That turned out to be illusory; it took nine more months before the end came, but I think that even if people could have foretold the future—the three-quarters of a year still left for many on Cyprus—they would still have danced; for the long-hoped-for-day, "the yearned-for hour" (as the song goes) had finally arrived.

Another hoped-for hour arrived: the day that the announcement concerning the closing of the camps came over the air. Bevin had finally given in. I heard the news over the radio and tried to contact Sir Godfrey Collins. I was unable to do so. It was nighttime and my chauffeur was not available; I went on foot to the Koenigsfelds, our employees who lived in Famagusta, to bring them the news and ask them to take me in their car to celebrate the event in camp.

It was about 9:30 in the evening. I rang the bell of the Koenigsfeld household and Cilly came to the door. In my excitement I told her, "Hurry up, get dressed and come to camp. The camps are closing." She went to call her husband. I later found out that she told her husband, "Laub is here. I think he's drunk. He says the camps are closing." Out came Kurt in pajamas and a stocking nightcap (the first time I had ever seen one). I convinced him that I was not drunk and that we ought to go to camp. This time it was a celebration in the mud again; it was the month of February and the rains had started. As on November 29th, mud did not stop anyone from expressing joy, and again the dancing and the celebrations went on all night. At last the yearned for hour had arrived.

Eventually, in a few days, Israeli boats came to take to Israel the 10,000 or so persons that were still in camp. I asked Josh Leibner, who together with his family had already been back in Ein Hashofet for some months, to come over to Cyprus and join Itzhak and me in accompanying the last boatload. We were given VIP treatment by the British. They too were relieved. They had not liked their work; at last the unpleasantness of being jailers, not of prisoners of war but of prisoners of government, was over.

A personal word will be forgiven, I hope. One day, during my preparation for the final departure, a delegation from the Central Committee came to see me to thank me for the JDC work and for what I had done personally: they presented me with a medal on which a verse from the Ecclesiastes was inscribed in Hebrew: "A good name is better than gold." I have received other honors on several occasions, but, though I have treasured them, nothing is as precious to me as that medal. I plan to pass it on to my sons with instructions that they in turn should pass it on to one of their children, and that it should forever remain in the family.

The reception in Israel was also an experience to remember. We arrived in Haifa. Thousands of people were there to welcome us, carrying banners and streamers, and waving flags. Among the thousands were many of the former deportees, now established citizens of Israel. The speeches seemed endless to me, but they were appropriate; for Israel, though at war, was gaining new citizens through the final closing of the last internment camp.

The Attitude of the British

The British on Cyprus were, of course, the implementers of the infamous policy of Ernest Bevin: deporting illegal immigrants—IJI's as the British called them. For the British the abbreviation meant Illegal Jewish Immigrants, and when I used the abbreviation letters, I told them I meant "Intercepted Jewish Immigrants."

Bevin had his malign policies. The army, the Palestine authorities, the Cyprus authorities, even the colonial office, were called on to implement those policies. From the outset, I must say, I quickly realized that a sharp distinction must be made between Bevin and the army people and others in Cyprus. While they and the Jews were presumably adversaries, most of the time it did not turn out to be so in practice. The army people—at least their commanders and others —acted conscientiously, yet obviously in a manner distasteful to them. As Colonel Widdicombe, the first supervisor of the camps told me, "This is no job for a soldier. I don't want to be the jailer of women and children."

I think it would be well to indicate by a specific example what I mean by this difference between the policy-maker Bevin and the policy-implementers in service. Take Major Newman, for instance, the commander of Camp 55, the first camp to receive internees. A man in his 50's, he was soft-spoken, military in his bearing, but utterly human and non-military in his attitude. In this case, I use the word "military" to imply rigidity, officiousness, strict discipline, and "non-military" as its opposite. Major Newman obviously was troubled by the fact that he had women and children in his camp. That was not what he had been trained for and he did whatever he could to help, even things he was not supposed to do: he increased the rations of milk and vegetables for his camp, knowing that it was a violation of the regulations. I knew about this and said nothing. In our working relationship, he surely sensed how much I appreciated what he did.

It was in this camp that the unfortunate demonstration which led to the death of Shlomo Chaimson at the gate took place, but Newman was not responsible. Another person, specifically charged with security in the camp, a very caricature of a British captain, gave the order. When the dead man was carried out on the shoulders of his comrades to the lorry which would take him to the Margoa cemetery, Major Newman stood at attention in silent respect for the deceased.

Two British sergeants, Clifford Martin and Melvyn Paice, were hanged by the Etzel group in Palestine (the group led by Begin) in retaliation for the shooting of Jewish soldiers. The kidnapping or the seizure of the sergeants made news all around the world for weeks and the hanging came as a great shock, though as an expected outcome. The liaison at camp at that time was a Mr. Smith, whom I met after the news of the hanging. He was curt, angry, and said something to me, implying that I was among those responsible, or that all of us were responsible in his eyes. I responded to Mr. Smith, "Aren't you confusing me with Palestinians? I am an American citizen. You know that I have as much to do with those affairs as you have, so please, I can understand your feelings, but don't vent them on me." He took my words in the spirit in which I said them, but our relations cooled off for the short period that he was to stay until his successor arrived.

The day of the hangings, I had to attend to matters in the Jewish wing of the BMH, the British Military Hospital. That, too, was behind barbed wire and in order to enter, one had to show an identification. A sergeant was in charge of supplies. It was he who brought, upon request, linens, bandages, and medical supplies to the nurses. The day of the hangings, when I saw him, he greeted me in his usual affable way and carried on his work. It was only later that I learned that he was a first cousin of one of the hanged soldiers, but that did not stop him from performing his duties.

Two colonels, supervisors of the camp, resigned because they could not do their work. The first was Colonel Widdicombe, a Cockney, a regular army soldier who rose through the ranks and did everything he could possibly do within the limits of his command to help us. I saw him almost daily in his office and very often I would sit on his desk and converse with him about camp matters. When we got to know each other a little better, we even talked about personal matters and one day Widdicombe told me that he'd had it. This was not his idea of army service and he asked to be transferred elsewhere. He was going to be married soon to one of the women soldiers under his command, and the JDC gave him a gift of a silver service when he left.

Colonel Dent, who succeeded him, felt the same way, though he was of a different stripe from Widdicombe. Dent was of upper-class origin. His English was beautiful, slow and accurate. He spent a good deal of his time in Xylotymbu, the so-called winter camps. Like the camps of Caraolos they were near the sea, but for security reasons nobody would be permitted to go into the sea to swim. Camp 64, one of the winter camps, had many children in it and in the hot summer months they looked longingly at the sea. I asked Colonel Dent to allow the children to bathe and swim. He couldn't, he said. His hands were tied. I didn't give in. I asked him again and again. Finally he agreed. Children were permitted to swim but, in looking back upon the incident, I remember how comical that was. Preceding the children was an armored tank with guns pointing at them and following the children was another armored tank with guns. This went on for a couple of days until the idea became too ludicrous. Children are children and the soldiers—perhaps some of them fathers—realized that they had children to control for soon many of the children were riding on the tanks. Dent, too, resigned in protest against what was happening on Cyprus.

A man who broke all rules and knew that he was breaking them was Captain Maitland. He became very friendly with Josh Leibner and would often visit him, telling him what was going on, which he should not have been talking about. He knew that the Leibners were occasionally hiding persons who escaped from the camps, and it was he who warned Leibner of a possible search. Among all his colleagues and those sympathetic to us, Maitland stands out as one of the *hasidei umot haolam*, whom our rabbis call "the righteous among the gentiles."

At the beginning of the Cyprus period, Judah Magnes, the president of the Hebrew University, was on the board of the Palestine JDC. In one of my first visits to Palestine after coming to Cyprus, I was sent to see Dr. Magnes and his wife at their home surrounded by a lovely garden in the Rehavia section of Jerusalem and I told him our story. Magnes asked me to come with him to see Sir Alan Cunningham, the High Commissioner in charge of the mandate, who dwelt in Government House, which was under special guard in those turbulent times. We were received cordially (evidently Magnes and he were good friends), and I poured out my story, protesting the incarceration and stressing the fact that neither food nor medical attention nor other amenities, officially provided by the British, were sufficient and that the JDC had to come to help out. He listened sympathetically, thanked Magnes and me for what the JDC was doing and promised to do what he could. Cunningham, according to what Dr. Magnes later told me, did write a sharp letter to the proper authorities in London, but to no avail. It was obvious in our talk that he was deeply troubled by the whole matter.

Sir Godfrey Collins deserves a special place. He was the third of the liaison between the British and us. He had been a top civil servant in India and was, I think, brought out of his retirement to take over the post in Cyprus. He was tall, in his 60's, lean, of few

100

"Going to the Beach." British tanks escort children going for a swim in the sea.

words, correct, and inscrutable. I never knew whether what I was saying made any impression on him personally or whether he was listening as a matter of duty, and his usual reply to my requests, unless it was for something that he could immediately act upon, was, "I'll look into it," or "I'll inquire." One of the matters that went on between him and me for months was my request for the building of a special house to take care of the many infants that needed attention. Two thousand infants were born in Cyprus, nearly all of them delivered at the BMH and then brought back to camp to be with their mothers. Our nurses and the special infant nurses, *metapelot*, as the Hebrew has it, insisted that a tent or a Nissen hut did not provide a good environment for infants and that an infant's home had to be built. I asked for a sketch of such a home, and I got it. It turned out to be quite a building, 100 feet by 40, with many windows, special cribs, special tables, the necessary closets for supplies, tables for medical examination—in sum, a rather expensive building. I brought this matter to the attention of Sir Godfrey Collins and got the usual, "I'll inquire." The nurses kept asking for it and I became more urgent in my demands. I warned Sir Godfrey of dire consequences, hundreds of infants possibly dying because of the failure to build this infant's home. Again the answer, "I'll inquire." Eventually, after some months of almost daily pressing, a positive response came and the house was built. It was so well done that our nurses said there was nothing like it even in Palestine.

After the camps closed many months later, I learned from Sir Godfrey that he wrote—he did not merely inquire, he wrote urgent letters—presenting my case as forcefully as possible as if it were his own. I am sure that it was his letters and his insistence which won the day for the infant's home.

One other person, the Colonial Minister Sir Arthur Creech Jones, needs to be mentioned. To sum up his attitude, here is a citation from Hansard, the official parliamentary record dated 2/17/49: "I also gratefully recognize the work of the American Joint Distribution Committee under their director, Mr. Laub, who spared neither pains nor expense in providing welfare staff and services for the detainees." I don't know whether it is typical or not of the British to thank others in the pursuit of their duties, but typical or no, Creech Jones did thank the JDC and me for our work. It sums up the attitude that other Englishmen, aside from Bevin, had towards us.

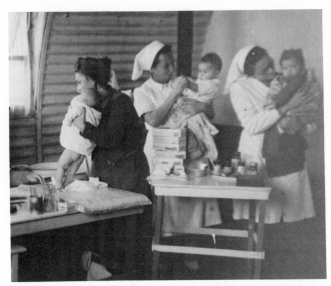

Infants are cared for in Caraolos Camp's "Station Milk Drop."

Sir Godfrey Collins speaking with camp *shokhet*.

Here is another example of British behavior, this time the attitude of the Governor of Cyprus. One of our early medical directors was Dr. Chaim Rappaport. When Dr. Rappaport came to the camp he was young, energetic, totally immersed in what he had to do as a doctor and, as I later discovered, also involved in clandestine matters with the *Haganah*. As a doctor, he was first rate. We all liked him. He treated not only the campers, but also the JDC staff and, in fact, he took care of me when I fell ill. He even treated some of the British who, at their request, asked that their wives be examined by Dr. Rappaport or any one of our own doctors. Of course we acceded to it, under the impression that even the British recognized that our medical service was superior to their own. Dr. Rappaport met his future wife in camp. She was a nurse. I only remember her first name, Lilka. She was a very pretty, dark-haired young woman, and in the course of their work she and Rappaport fell in love and were married in Cyprus, actually in our home in Famagusta.

I knew about some of Dr. Rappaport's activities, which were not absolutely according to Hoyle. For instance, prior to Lilka's coming to camp, he would take out from the camp a detainee who was a doctor herself and bring her openly to the Savoy Hotel to dances. I suppose the guards at the camp thought she was a JDC employee. She must have had some kind of identification card, probably forged, and though I knew about this, I felt that if they could get away with it, why not. Why shouldn't a person, a doctor who helped us, have the opportunity once in a while to come out freely to the city and enjoy herself?

Sometime in the summer of 1947 I was called in by the British and told that Dr. Rappaport could no longer have access into the camp. I protested vehemently, but fruitlessly. Realizing that I was getting nowhere with my protests, I decided to go to see the Governor of Cyprus and talk to him about it. The Government House was in Nicosia, but in summertime the government would move up to Mt. Troodos, a mountain 6,000 feet high, two hours away from Kyrania, one of the six major cities of Cyprus. The governor received me without much ado, offered me tea and then we talked and he told me that Rappaport must go, for there was evidence, undoubted evidence, that he was involved with whomever it was in camp who aided people to escape. To make his point more clearly, the governor showed me the dossier on Rappaport, and sure enough there were

104

reports after reports incriminating Rappaport in illegal activities. I had nothing to say to this. However, I pointed out to the governor that I knew nothing about this—and that was the truth—and that the people in the camp were terribly perturbed about Rappaport's explusion. I made the following proposal to the governor: I asked him to allow Rappaport to go back to the camp and I guaranteed to him that within two or three weeks, Dr. Rappaport would resign and leave. This was patently a face-saving device for me and, if you wish, for the British, and one designed to cool the temper of the internees. The governor agreed. Dr. Rappaport was re-installed as our physician and after several weeks it was announced that, owing to pressing medical matters in Palestine, he had to return there.

In thinking about this and talking it over with various persons, we came to two conclusions about this action of the Cyprus governor. First, he was an administrator and he considered me as an administrator, and he understood the problem that I was facing. Therefore, as one administrator to another, he was ready to help me out. Secondly, he, like other Britishers, didn't really like the whole idea of the camps; this was a matter forced upon him and as long as he could help, he helped.

One further word about the governor. When the camps closed, he asked me to come to the Government House, this time in Nicosia, and have lunch with him. After lunch, he spoke dispassionately about what he thought would be the problems facing the new government in Israel. He predicted that the government of Israel, because of its inexperience in governing, would soon fall apart, that the Arab world surrounding Israel would be victorious and that nothing good really would come out of Israel's independence. He said this to me without any trace of satisfaction in his voice or sympathy for the Israelis, merely as his seasoned judgment of what the situation was. He was wrong of course. We all know that; but he was like others described in this chapter, a Britisher with whom it was a pleasure to deal on delicate matters involving the camp.

Another instance which cost the British authorities quite a lot of money was an idea generated by Dr. Rosenzweig, then our chief dentist. He thought it was the army's duty, or the British duty, to make sure that all internees had good teeth. Whether it was right or not, I don't know, but it certainly would eventually save Israel and the internees themselves much money to have their dental needs

filled before arrival in the Promised Land. I presented the matter to Sir Godfrey, and very soon after my request was approved. The result of the agreement was the establishment of a dental clinic, with full dental equipment, four dental chairs and necessary accessories. The JDC brought over additional dentists who set to work on the campers. Teeth were repaired, fillings, inlays, even dentures were made and all of it was paid for by the British. I am sure that Sir Godfrey's approval of this request had a great deal to do with the final establishment of the clinic. I remember one amusing note. We always had four dentists in the clinic and at one time all the names of the dentists began with Rosen—Dr. Rosenzweig, Dr. Rosenthal, and two other Rosen something.

In summary, there were British and British and, as I attempted to show, a sharp line of difference must be drawn between Bevin and those who had to implement his decisions. I've often thought about their attitude and wondered. I've never arrived at any definite conclusion, aside from the obvious one that their humanitarian sense was aroused. Yet, in similar situations, in other countries and other armies, those feelings remained untouched.

One conclusion I have come to: if I had to be incarcerated in a camp, I would choose the British to be my keepers, not the French, of course not the Germans, possibly not even the Americans. The spark of humanity which women and children and other unfortunates in Cyprus kindled in them, is, I think, unique to the British army.

Scenes and Vignettes

My Four-Year-Old
Son Marc is Imprisoned

Marc, the younger of my two boys, was four years old and attended nursery school and kindergarten in the Caraolos Camp. I would drop him off at the gate every day on my way to the office right outside the camp. Marc's attending school in the camp together with the children who were interned became a matter much talked and wondered about. We felt that we needed the school and that the best place for our children would be in camp.

I would pick up my boys at lunchtime and come back with them after lunch for the rest of the day. One day on the way home for lunch, I stopped at the gates of Camp 55, expecting to see Marc waiting for me. I immediately presented myself to the security people, who didn't know me but called others who did, and Marc was released.

I asked my boy what happened and he told me that on his way out a new security man said to him, "Hey, kid, where are you going?" Marc said, "I'm going home." "Where do you come from, kid?" To which Marc replied, "New York." On hearing that from a four-year-old tot, the soldier placed Marc under guard in the security tent. Others who knew Marc talked to the security man, but, being new on his job, he was taking no chances. Everybody was amused and greeted my coming with laughter.

When the chief of security heard about it, he laughed too. To this day we are amused at the idea of four-year-old Marc being guarded by a soldier with a rifle, because he said he came from New York.

How I Discovered that I Could Drink

When I came to Cyprus I drank occasionally and had the *kiddush* wine, but drinking was not one of my habits. As soon as Charles Passman learned about my arrival, he told me that he would like to introduce me that evening to the British officers at their club. At nine that evening, Mr. Passman and I went there.

Located in a kind of enlarged hut, the club was nicely outfitted with a bar, sofas and chairs and various cozy corners where one could sit and chat. Passman made the rounds and introduced me. We exchanged the usual pleasantries and he and I sat down at a table.

The waiter placed a tumbler of ginger ale in front of us. I asked, "What's this?" Passman said, "It's scotch. You'd better drink it. This is a test." The sight of a tumbler full of scotch threw me into a dither. How could I ever finish a whole glass full of scotch? One reason for my violent distaste was that I was subject to occasional migraine headaches which would disable me for a day or so, and I was afraid of a hangover if I got drunk. But a test is a test. Passman told me I'd

better pass it if I was to be accepted as he hoped I would be, by the British. Having read enough mystery stories and having seen enough movies, I realized that the way to do it would be to nurse this big glass through the evening. From time to time I took a sip, made sure I had a pretzel or something else to eat, and after an interval not too long in the eyes of the observant British, I would take another sip. To my surprise, by the end of the evening I had finished the glass without getting drunk. In fact, Mr. Passman, about twenty years older than I, had some difficulty, and I helped him back to camp.

The lesson in drinking came in very handy. Thereafter, every Saturday night the British officers and I would gather at the Savoy bar. I would stand them to drinks and run up a bill of perhaps 50 pounds. Every farthing of it was worth it. I discovered that the average Britisher cannot drink much. Many a secret or at least many a tale which should not have been told to me was recounted merrily under the influence of liquor. I tried to remember everything I heard and, upon returning to my hotel room, I jotted down some notes and then passed them on to those in need of such information.

The ability to spend 50 pounds a week and to know how to drink turned out to be part of the necessary qualities of a JDC director on Cyprus.

My Children Think I Am Drunk

May 15th, 1948 marked the Declaration of Independence of the State of Israel. How it was celebrated in the camps has been described elsewhere. What I want to talk about is Saturday, the day after. I went into my office as usual. There were no sabbaths or holidays in the formal sense—work had to go on.

I was sitting in my office alone wondering what the declaration would mean, hoping it would hasten the closing of the camps. I honestly expected the camps to close within a week or so.

I was working when in walked one of the majors flanked by two captains. In his British accent he said, "Morris, today is a great day, don't you think? Shouldn't we celebrate?" I acted dumb and asked him what he meant. "Well, the State of Israel came into being yesterday. At last your state is independent." I continued to act dumb and reminded the major that I was an American, that while I

109

rejoiced in the independence of the state, it was not my state. However its independence did call for a celebration and so why not drink? I always had on hand Adom Atik and we began drinking. The major drank quickly, joyously, as bottle after bottle was emptied; his company captains also drank, but not as abundantly.

I also drank, perhaps more than usual, but it was a great occasion to celebrate, even if in the company of a British major. And this came after the tremendous celebration of the night before in the camp. When we parted, the major had practically to be carried out by his captains.

I don't drive. I had a car and chauffeur at my disposal and we drove home to my house at 11 Franklin Roosevelt Drive in Famagusta, a typical Middle Eastern home. Though there was no air conditioning in those days, it was cool in the summer and warm in the winter. This was achieved through a huge central foyer around which all the rooms were situated. The central foyer acted as an insulator against heat and cold, and even when the heat would reach 100 degrees, the house was relatively cool. The foyer was tiled in a lovely pattern, and part of the pattern was a series of straight lines running from one end to the other. I recall walking into the house and saying to Eve, Levi, and Marc, "I'm not drunk. Don't think I'm drunk. Here, I'll show you. I can walk a straight line." I began walking along one of the straight lines of the tiled floor and I made it, but both of my sons were convinced that they saw me drunk and so was my wife.

There is a Yiddish expression to the effect that "If the world says you're drunk, lie down." I don't know whether that expression came to my mind at the time, but I followed its advice and, protesting that I was not drunk, I went to sleep.

A Nine-Year-Old Deportee Declares His Party Affiliation

When a British boat arrived with deportees, they were met by a welcoming committee which invariably included members of various parties eager to welcome party members or to enlist new recruits. At one time as many as 17 parties were represented on Cyprus, not unusual to this very day in Israel.

One day, among those entering the registration room was an unaccompanied lad of nine, obviously an orphan, but already wise to

110

the ways of the world. Immediately upon entering the room he declared in Yiddish, "I am a member of the Left Zionist Workers Left." He used the Yiddish word "Linka" and its Hebrew equivalent "smol" for "left". We all laughed, but a party man eagerly registered the boy as a member of his party.

A Shameful Incident

One of the boats had to arrive on the Sabbath with several hundred people, and as usual the party welcomers were ready to receive them. For some reason or other, some of them began to quarrel. The quarrel soon turned into a fight and others joined in; they started throwing stones and whatever else was handy. There was nothing we could do to stop the uproar. We watched sadly and in great humiliation. The British were with us and we were ashamed of what was going on. More important than the British were the new arrivals, and the idea of their being welcomed by a group engaged in fighting one another was abhorrent. It had never happened before; it never happened again; yet it did take place and I cannot forget it. Neither could the emissaries and the members of the Central Committee and the welcomers themselves, who urgently called a meeting later to make sure that such a thing could never happen again.

A Woman's Paradise

Walking through the camp one day with Dr. Rappaport, we stopped to chat with a woman in advanced pregnancy and assured her that everything was going well. The woman was radiant. She was not only pretty, but in pregnancy absolutely beautiful, and she was all smiles at what Dr. Rappaport had to say. As we continued our stroll, the doctor turned to me and said, "You know, Moish, this is an ideal place for a woman to have a baby." I looked up in surprise and he continued, "Just think about it. Where else would a woman have medical attention at her beck and call any hour of the day and where else would a pregnant woman have her husband at her side all the time? Under normal conditions the husband is at work away from home, and the woman has to go to a clinic or a hospital or call her doctor if she feels the need to do so. Here none of this prevails. Believe it or not, this is a paradise for a pregnant woman." If this young woman's radiance was an attestation of his words, I had to believe it.

Gut Morgen, Frau Cohen

Even in camp under abnormal conditions, the desire to carry on life as usual becomes paramount. During the week internees would go about their tasks in shabby clothes, sometimes sloshing through the mud and acting as if they really were in a concentration camp.

But came the Sabbath for an observant Jew or Sunday for a non-observant Jew, and the appearance of the camp changed; the people themselves changed. The shabby clothes would disappear. People would stroll and visit with each other dressed up in the very best that they could find.

The following scene is etched in my mind, perhaps because it represents, in an exaggerated form, what a day of rest meant. It was a sloshy Sunday. It had rained for many days and as there were no paved roads to begin with, the usual hardened earth had turned into mud. The sun was now out and people were walking about. I remember seeing a well-dressed man wearing a fedora hat and carrying a cane (he evidently had been able to bring hat and cane with him from wherever he came) and every time he passed people he knew he would greet them with a "Good morning, Frau Cohen," "Good morning, Herr Levy." Each greeting was accompanied by his touching the fedora and by a low bow. He also greeted persons he didn't know, only then he omitted the name. As it turned out, this man saw Frau Cohen and Herr Levy and others every day, but Sunday was special—as if he was walking on the Kurfürstendamm in Berlin or any other main thoroughfare of the city he was familiar with, and simple civility called for the polite recognition of a passerby —the passion to be normal.

Pan Sailors Want Ice Cream

Many of the sailors of the Pan ships were Americans who had to stay in Cyprus for a while until their turn came, in spite of the fact that they were leaving sooner than others because they were sailors. Waiting even a short while was irksome: that was not what they had volunteered to do. They began to grumble, occasionally to act in an unpleasant manner, making demands that obviously could not be met. I decided to call them all together to a meeting. I didn't know their names; as far as I was concerned they were still the George Washingtons and the Thomas Jeffersons and the Charles de Gaulles and all the other fictitious names they had given upon arrival.

We sat on the grass in one of the camps, 30 or more people, and we talked matters over in English. I explained our situation and asked them to be understanding. I praised them for their bravery, told them how much we admired them for their voluntary efforts, and assured them that they would go as soon as the Central Committee and the *Mossad* men could organize their departure.

At first the talk was amicable, but then the grumbling started, and in a somewhat acerbic tone I asked, "What is it that you want?" And someone said, "Ice cream." With rather heavy-handed irony I retorted, "What flavor?" They mentioned the usual flavors: chocolate, vanilla, strawberry. In my displeasure I continued, "That's all? We have more. We have rum raisin and chocolate chip." I tried to remember as many of the Howard Johnson flavors as I could and reeled them off. For a moment they took me seriously, but then they caught on and began to cuss me out. I heard them use some four-letter words and I used some myself. The discussion grew tenser and finally I said, "You can all go to hell," and stalked off.

Not long afterwards they did leave and many of them continued their voluntary maritime activity for *Aliya Bet*. Some years later I met one of them, we recognized each other, embraced as if we were the best of friends, and discovered that he was now a citizen of Israel, an art dealer, promoting the works of Israeli artists, and a frequent visitor to the United States on behalf of his work. He told me that he remembered that incident in Caraolos and our unpleasant conversation, and he apologized for it. I assured him that no apologies were

113

necessary, that I understood, and that perhaps if I were in their place I would have acted the same way. It must have been extremely irksome to find oneself imprisoned behind barbed wire rather than out on the open sea or at a port in the Mediterranean helping refugees to board. He agreed, but apologized again, and told me more about some of those he remembered. A few were back in America, but many decided to become Israelis.

Chacun à son Goût

I received a cable one day which threw me into a joyous mood. Our New York office was sending powdered eggs and powdered milk in barrels for camp distribution. I realized that this was a coup in itself, for despite the many doors that were opened to the JDC, there were some things which it could not easily accomplish; among them was the acquisition of the much sought-after powdered eggs and powdered milk which the army needed. When they finally arrived, I had them distributed as quickly as possible to the camp, with instructions on how to use them. A few days later, in taking my usual tour of inspection, I was attracted by a game of soccer, the ubiquitous sport practiced by all Europeans, and I stood on the sidelines to watch. In following a ball, I noticed the boundaries of the area and to my horror discovered that the powdered eggs had been used to outline the fields.

I called for a meeting of the Central Committee immediately and I protested, but to no avail. "Whoever wanted this? It isn't fit for human consumption, and just because we are internees there is no reason why we have to use it." I explained to them that the powdered foods were used by the army, that all Allied armies were eager to receive them and how a good chef could do wonders with them. I recalled that Italian chefs made gourmet meals with powdered eggs. My words made no impression, and so New York's grandiose efforts were literally grounded into the dust of Cyprus.

Cyprus is primarily an agricultural island, though it is also well known for some mineral deposits, especially copper, hence the name Cyprus. Its chief agricultural crop is carob, which is not eaten by people but ground for use as cattle fodder and exported all over the world. The citrus products—oranges, grapefruit, lemons, limes

—are also a major export, and we supplemented the daily food ration with oranges. At the very beginning we gave out grapefruit, but no one would eat it—that's for animals, I was told, for cattle, not for human beings. I was sadly disappointed; the grapefruit was very good and it was cheap, less than a penny each.

Their refusal to eat grapefruit reminded me of an incident that happened to me when I visited Palestine for the first time in December, 1944. I was going through Degania, accompanied by an American woman who had settled there and who acted as my guide. As we passed an orange tree, she plucked a couple of oranges and gave them to me and later she plucked a grapefruit. I held the citrus fruits behind my back and kept walking when suddenly I felt someone tugging at the grapefruit. I turned around and was amused to see a lamb following me and nibbling.

The powdered milk and the grapefruit in Cyprus brought to mind the famous French saying, "Chacun à son goût." In speaking about this incident, I have often changed it to "Chacun à son *mishugas.*"

The British Decoration for a JDC Staffer

With the arrival of more and more ships, the Dekhelia camps grew steadily in number from Camp 64 through Camp 70. Because Camp 68 was across a public road from Camp 67, people could not mingle. The British decided to ease the situation so that people in the Dekhelia camps could really see each other, and they built a bridge between Camp 67 and Camp 68. The bridge was a covered one, guarded of course, and for a while it looked as if it would not be used because this covered bridge in Dekhelia resembled bridges in the Warsaw ghetto. For a while, perhaps a week, the bridge was boycotted and demonstrations took place on either side of the bridge; but finally the desire of people to see each other broke down the resistance and the bridge began to be used.

The bridge became a model for some of the artists and craftsmen among the internees because, together with the watchtowers, it symbolized imprisonment on Cyprus.

When the winter camps or those in Dekhelia began filling up, it became necessary to have always someone on the spot there. I asked Mr. Litwak of the Palestine office to find a suitable person to act as my deputy in charge of those camps. He found David Landwehr, who was appointed to the post.

Tall, erect, handsome, Landwehr was of Viennese origin, spoke perfect English, and, of course, Hebrew. He was married to a pediatrician, Edda, had served in the British Army, and was ready to take the post.

He was a good choice. He immediately established a good relationship not only with the staff in Dekhelia, and, more importantly, with the internees, but also with the British officers in charge there. He lived at camp, and soon became known for his habit of taking an ice-cold shower (there was no hot water) out in the open, every morning, regardless of the weather.

This braced him for the day, I suppose, and for his hard work. One day, not long after Landwehr's arrival, word was received by the government in Cyprus to search him out because he had been awarded an MBE for bravery in action, and was asked to come to Nicosia to the governor's mansion. We were very proud of Landwehr's recognition, but he tried to shake it off as nothing too important. Our pride also had a tinge of satisfaction in that one of our staff members, helping Jews interned by the British, was recognized by them, and their Army in particular, as worthy of recommendation to the Queen for this award. It was kind of cocking a snoot at the British, a way of saying to them, "See, look who is with us. Look who we are. Even you have to recognize, even you have to acknowledge our worth."

Sephardim and Sephardim

Jews are either of Ashkenazic or of Sephardic origin. Most European Jews—except those of southern European countries—are Ashkenazic, as are many millions from America, South Africa, South America, and Australia.

The Sephardic Jews (from the word "Sfarad" which means "Spain") are from North Africa, the Middle Eastern countries and southern Europe, including Spain, Italy, and the Balkans (Yugoslavia, Bulgaria, Greece, Turkey, Rumania). The population of Israel today is divided among those of Ashkenazic and Sephardic origin. A new term has come into being in Israel for the latter, namely *Edot Hamizrach*, Jews of the East, or Oriental Jews. The word "oriental" is not to be confused with the usual meaning of "oriental" and does not refer to Jews from the Far East, Japan or China, but rather to what we know as Sephardic Jews.

While all Jews have many religious matters in common, such as holidays, the Bible, and the Talmud, there are differences, sometimes narrow, between Ashkenazim and Sephardim. The prayer-books, while containing all basic prayers, do not necessarily follow the same order and some prayers, especially medieval, poetic liturgy, may appear in one and not in the other. In addition, Ashkenazic Jews originally spoke Yiddish (many still do), while many Sephardic Jews speak Arabic or Judeo-Arabic, Ladino, or similar tongues.

The words "Ashkenazic" and "Sephardic," while conveying these differences, are nevertheless umbrella terms, for within each of these communities there are additional differences in modes, rites, and other variations in ritual celebration or custom. Thus, for instance, the Italian rite is not quite the same as the Moroccan rite, and the Yemenite rite may be different from others. A Yemenite speaking Hebrew is unmistakably a Yemenite; his Hebrew is pronounced in a manner unlike that of anyone else; listening to a Yemenite is a joy to the ear.

Similarly, among the Ashkenazic there are differences, one of which is that within the Ashkenazic ritual there is a so-called Ashkenazic mode and a Sephardic mode. This Sephardic mode really has little to do with the true ritual of the Sephardim. Even within this Sephardic mode there are differences. One must be thoroughly at home with these matters to understand them. A lifetime of study could be devoted just to the variations in rite, mode and custom among Sephardim and Ashkenazim and the nuances of variation in each custom.

Nearly all the internees on Cyprus were of Ashkenazic origin, except for about 2,500 who came from the Balkan countries and North Africa. To minister to their special needs, and primarily to have a sense of kinship with one of their own, Elie Moyal was sent by the Mapai labor party of Palestine as an emissary to the Sephardim. He worked with them for many months. He still retains his interest in the Sephardim and has been a member of the Knesset, a Sephardi put forth by the Mapai party.

117

One day Moyal came to me and said that as the High Holidays were approaching, Sephardic prayerbooks ought to be supplied. I asked him how many we needed; he felt that 250 would be sufficient, so I requested our Palestine office to send them to us. In due time, they arrived. I called in Moyal and turned over the shipment to him, accompanied with a remark to the effect that I was happy that they came so fast; it was rather unusual for an order to be filled so quickly.

Moyal took the packages but quickly came back with a crestfallen face. "It's a mistake. Somebody made a mistake," he said. "These aren't Sephardic prayerbooks. These are Ashkenazic prayerbooks using the Sephardic mode." I cabled to Palestine to notify them of the error, but this time the usual lengthy delay between an order and its arrival did take place and the kind of prayerbook that Moyal needed came after the holidays.

It was not an obvious error for the Palestine office to send us Ashkenazic books in the Sephardic mode, for many Palestinian Jews used those prayerbooks, but it was an error nevertheless. Moyal did his best, and we all learned a lesson about Sephardim and Ashkenazim.

Looking Back

My reminiscences are finished—fortified by notes and letters of the time about which I write and by my references to books, newspapers and archives.

As I write these lines some three decades later, a few things stand out to me and some questions remain. The staff I had was outstanding. Work was not only work well done, but done beyond the call of duty. No one, not even the supervisors, had to apportion tasks or hours. No one paid attention to the clock or to the passing days. The only attention given to time was the seemingly endless time during which the internees had to stay behind barbed wire, deprived of freedom, and yearning to go on to Palestine. That goal, that intense desire, made them and our workers one, and made us unaware of time or of the many difficulties engendered by our tasks.

I was the supervisor of our welfare work and all that it encompassed, and of course I had help in my supervisory tasks. I cannot forget my colleagues—the doctors, nurses, social workers, educators, clerical workers, cooks—and especially one who was longest in Cyprus, Itzhak Yacobi. He reminds one of the relationship between Ralph Bunche and his superior, Folke Bernadotte. Yitzhak was the man who always remembered the rules, who followed them minutely and who could not be moved from his honesty and integrity. He kept reminding me of the rules and if occasionally I broke one, he understood and said nothing.

In Cyprus I, the former teacher, was called upon to face uncharted problems and to be not only a supervisor and administrator, but also a financier, a diplomat, a warehouse keeper, an arbiter among sailors and captains, an observer of the military. I also had to discuss with colonels and generals their strategy in keeping the so-called illegal Jewish immigrants behind barbed wire and often vigorously disagreed with them and their ways. I had to supply food, health amenities, clothing, as well as culture, education and entertainment. Moses Leavitt (the late secretary of the JDC), used to make speeches about the various roles that the JDC was called upon to perform in its fulfillment of the three R's—relief, rescue and rehabilitation—and his words were not mere rhetoric. Out in the field, we were suddenly taking on tasks for which there was no training. Only common sense guided us and only devotion to Jews inspired us. We made mistakes, but more often than not we rose to the occasion and emerged victorious. I am reminded of the time, when I taught among my other chores as a Hebrew teacher, Bar Mitzvahs. Sometimes I had a boy who didn't read Hebrew well, could not carry a tune, or speak articulately. And I used to wonder how he would make it on the Sabbath of his Bar Mitzvah. The Sabbath came, and lo, the lad read correctly, sang fairly well, and spoke clearly. He rose to the occasion. He was not an embarassment nor did he fail.

One of the problems that stand out in my reminiscences is that I was alone. I had colleagues, but they were my subordinates; that is, while being as frank and as straightforward as possible, they were naturally constrained, and policy-making decisions were ultimately mine. I could not talk everything over with Joe Schwartz—he was in Paris or on a trip to the field—nor with any other country director. Often I had to make decisions on the spot, but the consequences and thoughts lingered long afterwards. This loneliness was mitigated, it is true, by annual country directors' conferences, but these were not enough. I felt, most of the time, alone on an island, literally and figuratively, and had to fend for myself. Joe Schwartz understood this and overlooked mistakes and applauded victories; so did my colleagues. But the feeling of isolation nevertheless gnawed one's bones intensively enough to be remembered even now.

A question that has been uppermost in my mind is that of the Sephardim. Cyprus was the first place where Ashkenazi Palestinians and, later, Israelis met them. They were not many, but they were the harbingers of waves of immigration which radically reduced the Jewish population of the countries of North Africa, Iraq, and other Arab lands. We made mistakes—the fiasco of wrong prayerbooks for them is an example—but did we learn from the mistakes? Did Israel? They represented a culture different from that of the Ashkenazis and within that culture there were nuances, shades, colorations and differing emphases, just as there are among Ashkenazis. But all were treated as persons with one common goal—Palestine.

Is that enough? Should not attention also be paid to their history, their dispersion among often hostile neighbors, their brand of piety, their ways? Integration is what one wants, but should it mean homogenization? I think, too, that some of the lessons of Cyprus could have helped Israel in welcoming them and making them feel more worthwhile as citizens.

I was an observer of and sometimes a participant in the making of history. The observer from the outside reads the facts as they are presented to him. His thoughts are based on what he considers the facts to be, yet it often turns out that they were not the facts. His thoughts were based on distortions. The public may have an image quite different from the truth. The hunger strikes by the internees which I described are an example. What the world has is a perception which sometimes does not match reality, and the perception may give rise to an ideology. The case of the Pan ships and the British foreign office and George C. Marshall's belief that the immigrants they brought were all Communists or Communists' agents is another example. After all, they did come from Bulgaria, and carried a contingent of Bulgarians as well as thousands of Rumanian Jews. Bulgaria and Rumania were Communist countries. Both Bulgaria and Rumania let these Jews go. Ergo, these Jews were Communists.

That was the perception. The reality was different. Yet it took a long time to shed this perception and its ensuing ideology in the face of reality. Is not the same thing repeated today? Perception, ideology, reality—all get mixed up and it takes a long time to unscramble them.

When I read or hear about others who act oddly or seemingly treacherously, I remember my initiation on Cyprus. And I am in conflict with myself because I did do the British bidding in the hope of preventing the use of tear gas; should I instead have refused to do their bidding and let them remove the human cargo by themselves in their own way? After all, they made only a request, but could not order me to fulfill it. Because I did do the British bidding I was labeled a traitor. For the Jews in the hold, I was not even under orders; I was merely acting on a request. Being under orders is today generally not even accepted as an excuse—at best as an explanation, and the two are not synonymous. Perhaps the *Rafiah* Jews were right, for they saw me do the British bidding and so in their eyes I acted as a traitor. Yet I know in the inner recesses of my being that I was not a traitor. And I know that if the Jews involved had known the true situation, they would agree with me.

In reading these reminiscences, could one arrive at the conclusion that the Cyprus camps were fun? They certainly were not. They were exciting, but that is not synonymous with joy. The internees suffered pain, they were sorrowful, and they were defiant. Our workers and I tried to alleviate, if possible to eliminate, the pain, reduce the sorrow, and bolster the morale of the internees by showing them that the world was thinking of them and fighting for them. Perhaps we succeeded. Many think we did. Cyprus became to the internees *Erev Eretz Israel*, the eve before Israel, laborious yet hopeful anticipation, supposedly wasteful but *davka*, full of learning and preparation for arrival and settlement in Israel. And for those of us who helped, it was ennobling to live through it all. For me, personally, it was the most exciting period of my life.

AFTERWORD

I came to Cyprus in 1947 on behalf of the Bezalel School of Fine Arts where I had just completed a very successful first year of teaching. I had to create a school out of nothing. It was decided by the management of the seminar that we had room for only 35 students, and we found there were many more applicants; it was hard to refuse many gifted and eager young people (most of whom were older than I).

The heat was so great that lessons had to start at six in the morning and to stop at eleven a.m. I can still remember how moved I was when every morning *all* the students were waiting as I arrived exactly on time. We spoke Yiddish which turned during the discourse into German, a language which came more naturally to me. One subject was the great revolution of Impressionist art. During the next six months, we enlarged the school into many departments of arts and crafts and all the students who wanted to could take part. Other teachers were recruited from the artists I knew in the camps and some were brought from Palestine. We studied linocutting and printing and we also had a bookbinding class. We decided to print an album of our life in the camps, and to publish it ourselves.

I consider my stay in Cyprus as my greatest pedagogical success which I attribute to my complete identification with my students whom I regarded as brothers and sisters. My teaching experience on Cyprus was one I will never forget. It was in the fullest sense a work of love.

Naftali Bezem

List of Boats

Name	Country of Embarcation	Date Sailed	Arrival on Cyprus	Passengers	Countries of Origin
1. *Yagur*	France	07/29/46	08/14/46	754	Poland and others
2. *Henrietta Szold*	Greece	07/03/46	08/14/46	536	Greece and Hungary
3. *Katriel Yaffe*	Italy	07/30/46	08/18/46	601	Poland and Rumania
4. *Kaf-Gimel Yordei Hasira*	Italy	08/02/46	08/18/46	790	Poland and others
5. *Arbah Heruyot*	Italy	08/23/46	09/04/46	1,015	Poland and others
6. *Palmach*	Italy	09/11/46	09/23/46	614	Poland
7. *Bracha Fuld*	Italy	10/09/46	10/21/46	806	Poland, Rumania, Hungary
8. *Latrun*	France	10/19/46	11/02/46	1,252	Poland and others
9. *Knesset Yisrael*	Yugoslavia	11/08/46	11/27/46	3,845	Rumania
10. *Rafiah*	Yugoslavia	11/26/46	12/12/46	785	Rumania
11. *Lanegev*	France	01/18/47	02/17/47	647	Poland
12. *Hama'apil Ha'almoni*	France	02/03/47	02/17/47	796	Poland
13. *Chaim Arlosoroff*	Sweden	01/27/47	02/28/47	1,348	Poland and Germany
14. *Ben Hecht*	France	02/22/47	03/10/47	626	Poland, France, Tunis
15. *Shabbatai Lozinsky*	Italy	03/04/47	03/13/47	848	Poland
16. *Moledet*	Italy	03/23/47	03/30/47	1,563	Poland
17. *Theodor Herzl*	France	04/01/47	04/15/47	2,641	Poland and Hungary
18. *Shear Yashuv*	Italy	04/06/47	04/23/47	768	Poland
19. *Hatikva*	Italy	05/08/47	05/17/47	1,414	Poland and others
20. *Mordei Hagettaot*	Italy	05/13/47	05/25/47	1,457	Poland
21. *Yehudah Halevi*	Algeria	05/10/47	05/31/47	460	North Africa
22. *Shivat Tzion*	Algeria	07/16/47	07/28/47	411	North Africa
23. *Yud-dalet Chalalei Gesher-haziv*	Italy	07/16/47	07/29/47	685	Poland and others
24. *Af-al-pi*	Italy	09/15/47	09/27/47	434	Poland and others
25. *Geula*	Bulgaria	09/26/47	10/02/47	1,388	Rumania
26. *Medinat Hayehudim*	Bulgaria	09/26/47	10/02/47	2,644	Rumania

Name	Country of Embarcation	Date Sailed	Arrival on Cyprus	Passen-gers	Countries of Origin
27. *Kadima*	Italy	11/05/47	11/16/47	792	Poland, Rumania, Hungary
28. *Lo-Tafchidunu*	Italy	12/11/47	12/24/47	884	Poland, Rumania, Hungary
29. *Kaf-tet b'november*	Corsica	12/14/47	12/29/47	680	Rumania, Hungary, North Africa
30. *Atzmaut (Pan Crescent)*	Bulgaria	12/26/47	01/01/48	7,612	Rumania and Bulgaria
31. *Kibbutz Galuyot (Pan York)*	Bulgaria	12/26/47	01/01/48	15,557	Rumania
32. *Lamed-Hei Giborei Kfar Etzion*	Italy	01/16/48	02/01/48	274	Rumania, Hungary, Poland
33. *Yerushalayim Hanetzura*	Italy	02/03/48		670	Rumania, Hungary, Poland
34. *Lakomemiut*	France	02/08/48	02/20/48	699	Countries of Europe, North Africa
35. *Bonim Velochamim*	Yugoslavia	02/18/48	02/28/48	1,002	Bulgaria
36. *Yechiam*	Italy	03/09/48	03/28/48	767	Hungary and others, North Africa
37. *Tirat Zvi*	Italy	04/03/48	04/12/48	798	Various countries
38. *Mishmar Haemek*	France	04/14/48	04/24/48	788	Various countries
39. *Nachshon*	France	04/14/48	04/26/48	553	Various countries
Total				52,221	

This list is adapted from David Schaary's, *The Cyprus Detention Camps.*

All the boats were given Hebrew names, though originally they bore other names. All boats were known to us by their Hebrew names, with the exception of the *Atzmaut* and the *Kibbutz Galuyot*, which were usually called by their original names, the *Pan Crescent* and the *Pan York*. The Hebrew names commemorated famous people, such as Theodor Herzl; kibbutzim, such as Mishmar Haemek; events, such as *Kaf-Tet B'november* (November 29, the date in 1947 when the U.N. voted to approve the partition of Palestine); Zionist ideas, such as *Shivat Tzion* (Return to Zion); or slogans such as *Lo Tafchidunu* (You shall not frighten us).

SELECTED BIBLIOGRAPHY

Bauer, Yehuda, *From Diplomacy to Resistance*, The Jewish Publication Society, Philadephia, 1970.

Bauer, Yehuda, *American Jewry and the Holocaust*, Wayne State University Press, Detroit, 1981.

Kimche, J&D, *The Secret Roads—The Illegal Migration of a People*, 1938-1948, Secker & Warburg, London, 1964.

Morse, Arthur D., *While Six Million Died*, Random House, New York, 1973.

Stone, I.F., *Underground to Palestine*, Published by Boni & Gaer, New York, 1946, republished by Pantheon, New York, 1978.

Itzhak, Ben-Yosef, *Michtavim Mekafrisin*, Sifriyat Tarmil, Tel-Aviv, 1973. Hebrew. Letters from one of the first emissaries on Cyprus.

Gruber, Ruth, *Destination Palestine*, Current Books, New York, 1948.

To my knowledge, the only complete published historical account of the internment on Cyprus is *Gerush Kafrisin*, written in Hebrew by David Schaary and published by *Hasifriya Haziyonit*, Jerusalem, 1981. It was also given the English title, *The Cyprus Detention Camps for Jewish "Illegal" Immigrants to Palestine, 1946-49*. Dr. Schaary was formerly an emissary to the *Noar Zioni* groups on Cyprus and spent a year there. His book is an historical account of the internment, a description of the camps, and a discussion of the social organization of the internees themselves. It includes many tables and documents.

PASS 386.

The bearer is permitted to enter the

prohibited area(s) of ....

ALL ITI CAMPS.

for the purpose of ....

DIRECTOR OF AJDC.

~~between sunrise and sunset~~ ALL HRS/OR.

~~at any hour~~ *(delete as required).* 2 SUNSET 7 of
2 1/04/48

Date 25 February 1948

(Sign.)
Defence   Security   Officer,   Cyprus.

See reverse for renewals.

Name Morris LAUB,

Address Famagusta.

Description

4454 PP&TJ 1 9.47

Morris Laub was born in Przemysl, Poland, June 23, 1909. Five years later his family emigrated to the United States. Living in the heart of the transplanted Jewish European culture of New York City's lower East Side, Morris was immediately placed into a *cheder* and at the age of nine into a yeshiva. A lively young scholar, his Bar Mitzvah speech was a "talmudic *pilpul*." At 17, he taught his first Hebrew school class and at 19 became a principal. In the early 1930's he was co-editor and co-publisher of the *Young Maccabbee*, a monthly magazine for Hebrew school children.

After having received degrees from both the City College of New York and the Teachers Institute of Yeshiva University, he continued his career of teaching, entering the New York High School system as one of its first teachers of Hebrew.

127

In 1944 he began his 12 year association with the American Joint Distribution Committee. After a stint in Paris, he was appointed JDC country director for Greece. In December, 1947 Laub became country director on Cyprus. He then went on to work at the European JDC headquarters in Paris and returned to New York in 1951 as assistant director of the JDC. For his work in the Cyprus camps, he was cited by the British House of Commons in 1947 and later by the Israeli Government in 1973.

In the late 1950's, he became director of the Social Action Committee of the United Synagogue of America and executive director of the World Council of Synagogues. He joined the board of YIVO Institute for Jewish Research in the early 1970's and in 1976 was chosen to be executive director and chairman of the board, a post he held until retirement in 1982.

Widowed twice, he has two sons, Levi and Marc, five grand-children and two step-grandchildren. Now retired and living in Berkeley, Laub is busy teaching classes in Yiddish grammar and literature, listening to music and continuing his scholarly searching.